The Ultimate Joke Book

p

This is a Parragon Book
First published in 2002

Parragon
Queen Street House
4 Queen Street
Bath
BA1 1HE, UK

Produced by Magpie Books, an imprint of
Constable & Robinson Ltd, London

Copyright © Parragon 2002

ISBN 0-75259-029-4

A copy of the British Library Cataloguing-in-Publication Data
is available from the British Library

Printed and bound in Dubai

Introduction

If you're a fan of silly jokes, you've come to the right place. *The Ultimate Joke Book* is packed to the gills with quirky quips and loony laughs. If you're wondering why the vampire gave up acting, what you get if you cross an orange with a comedian or what a snake's favorite game is, you'll find all the answers in this book.

If it's knock knock jokes you're after, open up to find Fletcher stick, Haden in the bushes and Isabella ding dong. You'll soon be doubling up with laughter at this crazy collection.

What happened when two vampires went mad?
They went bats.

Why do demons and ghouls get on so well?
Because demons are a ghoul's best friend.

What do you get if you cross a skeleton with a famous detective?
Sherlock Bones.

What trees do ghouls like best?
Ceme-trees.

What did the baby ghost eat for dinner?
A boo-loney sandwich.

☆   ☆   ☆

How can you tell if a corpse is angry?
It flips its lid.

☆   ☆   ☆

Where do undertakers go in October?
The Hearse of the Year Show.

☆   ☆   ☆

How do undertakers speak?
Gravely.

What keeps ghouls cheerful?
The knowledge that every shroud has a silver lining.

Why are graveyards so noisy?
Because of all the coffin.

When can't you bury people who live opposite a graveyard?
When they're not dead.

What was written on the hypochondriac's tombstone?
"I told you I was ill."

How did the glamorous ghoul earn her living?
She was a cover ghoul.

Why are cemeteries in the middle of towns?
Because they're dead centers.

What do young ghosts write their homework in?
Exorcise books.

Why did the mummy leave his tomb after 3,000 years?
Because he thought he was old enough to leave home.

How did the ghost song-and-dance act make a living?
By appearing in television spooktaculars.

Knock knock.
Who's there?
Aaron.
Aaron who?
Aaron on the chest means strength
   in the arms.

☆   ☆   ☆

Knock knock.
Who's there?
Aaron.
Aaron who?
Aaron'd boy, of course!

Knock knock.
Who's there?
Abba.
Abba who?
Abba'out turn!
Quick march!

☆   ☆   ☆

Knock knock.
Who's there?
Abel.
Abel who?
Abel to see you, ha, ha!

☆   ☆   ☆

Knock knock.
Who's there?
Abel.
Abel who?
Abel to go to work.

☆   ☆   ☆

What did the papa ghost say to the baby ghost?
Fasten your sheet belt.

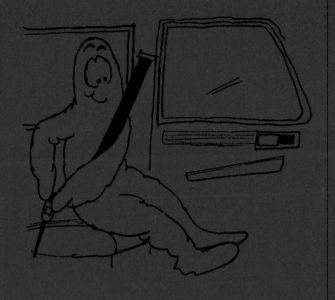

What did an embalmer of mummies say when he was asked how he kept the bodies so young?
"Tell them about the honey, mummy."

Why were ancient Egyptian children confused?
Because their daddies were mummies.

What do you call a ghost's mother and father?
Transparents.

☆   ☆   ☆

What kind of girl does a mummy take on a date?
Any old girl he can dig up.

☆   ☆   ☆

What kind of jewels do ghosts wear?
Tombstones.

☆   ☆   ☆

First Witch: My beauty is timeless.
Second Witch: Yes, it could stop a clock.

☆   ☆   ☆

Where do mummies go if they want to swim?
The Dead Sea.

What are little ghosts dressed in when it rains?
Boo-ts and ghoul-oshes.

Why are ghosts bad at telling lies?
Because you can see right through them.

What did the mother ghost say to her son?
"Don't spook until you're spooken to."

Who writes ghost jokes?
Crypt writers.

☆　☆　☆

What did the ghost teacher say to her class?
"Watch the board and I'll go through it again."

☆　☆　☆

What kind of street does a ghost like best?
A dead end.

☆　☆　☆

What happened when a ghost asked for a brandy at his local bar?
The landlord said, "Sorry, we don't serve spirits."

☆　☆　☆

What happened when the ghosts went on strike?
A skeleton staff took over.

☆　☆　☆

Knock knock.
Who's there?
Adder.
Adder who?
Adder you get in here?

Knock knock.
Who's there?
Ahab.
Ahab who?
Ahab to go to the bathroom in a
    hurry, open the door quick!

Knock knock.
Who's there?
Ahmed.
Ahmed who?
Ahmed a big mistake coming here!

Knock knock.
Who's there?
Aida.
Aida who?
Aida whole box of chocolates and I
    feel really sick.

Knock knock.
Who's there?
Aida.
Aida who?
Aida whole village cos I'm a
    monster.

Where do ghosts go on holiday?
The Ghosta Brava.

☆　☆　☆

How do you make a ghoul float?
Two scoops of ice cream, a bottle of
Coke and a slice of ghoul.

What do ghosts dance to?
Soul music.

☆　☆　☆

What is a ghost-proof bicycle?
One with no spooks in it.

☆　☆　☆

When do ghosts play tricks on each
other?
On April Ghoul's Day.

☆　☆　☆

What do ghosts say when a girl
soccer player is sent off?
Ban-she, ban-she!

☆　☆　☆

How do ghosts learn songs?
They read the sheet music.

☆　☆　☆

What do ghosts see at the theater?
A phantomime.

☆　☆　☆

Why did the ghost go to the
amusement park?
He wanted to go on the rollerghoster.

☆　☆　☆

This woman wanted to marry a ghost.
I can't think what possessed her.

Where do ghosts live?
In dread-sits.

What is a ghost's favorite bird?
A scare crow.

Why were the ghosts wet and tired?
They had just dread-ged the lake.

☆   ☆   ☆

What happened to the poverty-
stricken ghost?
He was dread-bare.

☆   ☆   ☆

What do ghosts eat?
Dread and butter pudding.

What's a skeleton's favorite musical
instrument?
A trom-bone.

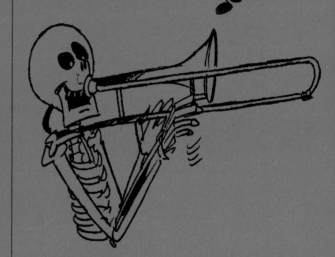

What do drunken ghosts drink?
Methylated spirit.

Why did the ghost work at Scotland
Yard?
He was the Chief In-Specter.

Knock knock.
Who's there?
Alaska.
Alaska who?
Alaska the teacher if I can leave the room.

☆ ☆ ☆

Knock knock.
Who's there?
Albert.
Albert who?
Albert you'll never guess.

Knock knock.
Who's there?
Aldo.
Aldo who?
Aldo the washing-up tonight.

☆ ☆ ☆

Knock knock.
Who's there?
Alec.
Alec who?
Alec your sister but I don't like you.

☆ ☆ ☆

Knock knock.
Who's there?
Aleta.
Aleta who?
Aleta bit of lovin'.

☆ ☆ ☆

Who is the most powerful ghoul?
Judge Dread.

What is the ghosts' favorite quiz
game?
Oooooo do you do.

What did the stupid ghost do?
He used to climb over walls.

Why don't you get locks on cemetery
gates?
There's no point – all the ghosts have
skeleton keys.

What do you call an owl with a
toupee?
Hedwig.

Why are ghosts at their loudest in
August?
Because they're on their howlidays.

What do ghosts write with?
Phantom pens.

What happened to the ghostly
fishmonger?
He sold his sole to the devil.

What's the definition of a skeleton?
Bones with the person scraped off.

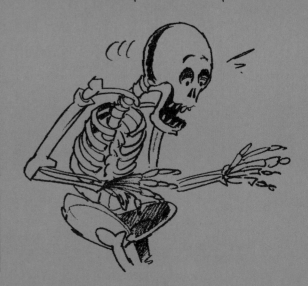

What do you call the ghost who is a child-rearing expert?
Dr Spook.

Where do ghosts live?
In a terror-tory.

What do you call a prehistoric ghost?
A terror-dactyl.

Doctor, doctor, I keep thinking I'm an invisible ghost.
Did someone say something?

What is the ghosts' favorite song?
Ooooo's that knocking at my door?

☆ ☆ ☆

How do you know you are haunted by a parrot?
He keeps saying, "Oooo's a pretty boy then?"

☆ ☆ ☆

How do ghosts like their drinks?
Ice ghoul.

☆ ☆ ☆

Where do ghosts get an education?
High s-ghoul.

☆ ☆ ☆

Which airway do ghouls fly with?
British Scareways.

Knock knock.
Who's there?
Alexander.
Alexander who?
Alexander friend want to come over.

Knock knock.
Who's there?
Alf.
Alf who?
Alf all if you don't catch me!

Knock knock.
Who's there?
Aleta.
Aleta who?
Aleta from your bank manager.

Knock knock.
Who's there?
Alf.
Alf who?
Alf way home.

Knock knock.
Who's there?
Alex.
Alex who?
Alex plain later if you let me in.

Woman in bed: Aaagh! Aaagh! A ghost just floated into my room!
Ghost: Don't worry, madam, I'm just passing through.

What kind of ghoul has the best hearing?
The eeriest.

How do ghouls like their eggs cooked?
Terrifried.

What do ghosts eat for dinner?
Ghoulash.

☆   ☆   ☆

What do ghouls eat for breakfast?
Dreaded wheat.

☆   ☆   ☆

What's a ghost's favorite day of the week?
The one before Saturday, because it's Frightday.

☆   ☆   ☆

Where do American ghosts go on holiday?
Lake Eerie.

☆   ☆   ☆

What kind of ghosts haunt operating theaters?
Surgical spirits.

Which ghost ate too much porridge?
Ghouldilocks.

What's a ghost's favorite dessert?
Knickerbocker Ghouly.

What's a ghost's favorite work of art?
A ghoulage.

What song does a ghost sing to warn people that he's around?
"Beware My Ghoulish Heart."

☆ ☆ ☆

What's a ghost's favorite Beatles' song?
"The Ghoul on the Hill."

☆ ☆ ☆

Which ghost was president of France?
Charles de Ghoul.

☆ ☆ ☆

Who's the most important member in the ghosts' soccer team?
The Ghoulie.

What should gymnasts do if they find themselves in a haunted house?
Exorcise.

Which ghost sailed the seven seas looking for rubbish and blubber?
The ghost of BinBag the Whaler.

Knock knock.
Who's there?
Amanda.
Amanda who?
Amanda the table.

Knock knock.
Who's there?
Amber.
Amber who?
Amberter than I was yesterday.

Knock knock.
Who's there?
Amber.
Amber who?
Amber-sting to go to the bathroom!

☆   ☆   ☆

Knock knock.
Who's there?
Althea.
Althea who?
Althea in court.

Knock knock.
Who's there?
Alvin.
Alvin who?
Alvin zis competition – just vait and
    see!

What's the result of smoking too much?
Coffin.

What do ghosts wear on wet days?
Caghouls.

What ghost is handy in the kitchen?
A recipe spook.

How does a ghost start a letter?
"Tomb it may concern."

Why didn't the skeleton go to the party?
He had no body to go with.

Ghost: Do you believe in the hereafter?
Phantom: Of course I do.
Ghost: Well, hereafter leave me alone.

If a skeleton rings your doorbell is he a dead ringer?

Why did the skeleton go to hospital?
To have his ghoul stones removed.

First Ghoul: Am I late for dinner?
Second Ghoul: Yes, everyone's been
eaten.

Why did the skeleton run up a tree?
Because a dog was after his bones.

How does a skeleton call his friends?
On a telebone.

Which skeleton wore a kilt?
Bony Prince Charlie.

☆　　☆　　☆

What is a skeleton's favorite drink?
Milk – it's so good for the bones.

☆　　☆　　☆

What do you call a skeleton that won't
get up in the morning?
Lazy bones.

☆　　☆　　☆

Why did the skeleton stay out in the
snow all night?
He was a numbskull.

☆　　☆　　☆

What do you call a stupid skeleton?
Bonehead.

☆　　☆　　☆

What happened to the skeleton that
stayed by the fire all night?
He was bone dry.

☆　　☆　　☆

Knock knock.
Who's there?
Anais.
Anais who?
Anais cup of tea.

Knock knock.
Who's there?
Andrew.
Andrew who?
Andrew a picture on the wall.

Knock knock.
Who's there?
Andy.
Andy who?
Andy man.

Knock knock.
Who's there?
Abbott.
Abbott who?
Abbott time you opened this door.

Knock knock.
Who's there?
Ann.
Ann who?
Ann amazingly good joke.

What happened to the lazy skeleton?
He was bone idle.

☆　☆　☆

Why do you have to wait so long for a ghost train to come along?
They only run a skeleton service.

☆　☆　☆

Who speaks at the ghosts' press conference?
The spooksperson.

☆　☆　☆

How do you make a skeleton laugh?
Tickle his funny bone.

☆　☆　☆

What sort of soup do skeletons like?
One with plenty of body in it.

☆　☆　☆

What happened to the boat that sank in the sea full of piranha fish?
It came back with a skeleton crew.

☆　☆　☆

First Ghoul: You don't look too well today.
Second Ghoul: No, I'm dead on my feet.

☆　☆　☆

Did you hear about the skeleton that couldn't jump out of the plane?
He had no guts.

☆　☆　☆

Some book titles:

Ghost Stories – by I.M. Scared

Going On A Witch Hunt – by Count Miout

I Saw a Witch in the Mirror – by Douglas Cracked

Boo! – by Terry Fied

Black Magic – by Sue Pernatural

A Ghost in my House – by Olive N. Fear

A Houseful of Ghouls – by Roxie Horror

What do ghosts like in their coffee?
Evaporated milk.

NOT THERE!

Did you hear about the ghost comedian?
He was booed off stage.

☆　☆　☆

It is a terrible night and Greg the Ghoul is out playing in it. There's thunder and lightning and all the graves are opening and all the nasty things that ever there were are wandering the earth.
Question: What did Greg's mother say?
Answer: "Come in, Greg."

☆　☆　☆

Did you hear about the ghost who learned to fly?
He was pleased to be back on terror-firma.

☆　☆　☆

Did you hear about the Italian ghost?
He liked spooketti.

Knock knock.
Who's there?
Apple.
Apple who?
Apple the door myself.

Knock knock.
Who's there?
April.
April who?
April will make you feel better.

Knock knock.
Who's there?
Argo.
Argo who?
Argo to piano lessons after school.

Knock knock.
Who's there?
Armageddon.
Armageddon who?
Armageddon out of here quick.

Knock knock.
Who's there?
Army Ant.
Army Ant who?
Army Ants coming for tea then?

What do you get if you cross a ghost
with a packet of potato chips?
Snacks that go crunch in the night.

Knock knock.
Who's there?
Harry.
Harry who?
Harry up! There's a ghoul after us!

Knock knock.
Who's there?
Scott.
Scott who?
Scott a nasty look about it, this place.
Is it haunted?

Knock knock.
Who's there?
Ellen.
Ellen who?
Ellen all the ghouls are
after me.

Knock knock.
Who's there?
Enid.
Enid who?
Enid some shelter from the ghouls.

Knock knock.
Who's there?
Olive.
Olive who?
Olive in a haunted house.

Knock knock.
Who's there?
Twyla.
Twyla who?
Twylight is when the vampires and ghoulies come out to play.

Knock knock.
Who's there?
Alistair.
Alistair who?
Alistairs in this house creak really spookily.

Knock knock.
Who's there?
Glasgow.
Glasgow who?
Glasgow away from this place – it's scary!

Knock knock.
Who's there?
Kyoto.
Kyoto who?
Kyoto the priest before the ghoulies get you.

Knock knock.
Who's there?
Havana.
Havana who?
Havana spooky old time!

Knock knock.
Who's there?
Atomic.
Atomic who?
Atomic ache is hard to stomach.

Knock knock.
Who's there?
Attila.
Attila who?
Attila you no lies.

Knock knock.
Who's there?
Audrey.
Audrey who?
Audrey to pay for this?

Knock knock.
Who's there?
Aardvark.
Aardvark who?
Aardvark a million miles for one of
    your smiles.

Knock knock.
Who's there?
Augusta.
Augusta who?
Augusta wind will blow the witch
    away.

Ghost: Doctor I want to go on a diet.
Doctor: Why do you want to do that?
Ghost: Because I want to keep my ghoulish figure.

Skeleton: Doctor, doctor, I feel like I've broken every bone.
Doctor: Well be glad you're not a herring.

A butler came running into his master's office. "Sir, sir, there's a ghost in the corridor. What shall I do with him?"
Without looking up from his work the master said, "Tell him I can't see him."

☆   ☆   ☆

What do you call a ghost's mistake?
A boo-boo.

☆   ☆   ☆

A workman had just finished laying a carpet in a witch's house when he realized he had lost his sandwiches. Looking around he saw a lump under the carpet. Not wanting to pull the carpet up again he just got a plank of wood and smashed the lump flat. Then the witch came into the room with a cup of tea for him. "Here's your tea," she said. "My you've laid the carpet well. Just one thing, though. Have you seen my pet toad anywhere?"

Witch: What day is it?

Wizard: Halloween.

Witch: Yes, hello to you to, Ivan, but what day is it?

A man was staying in a big old country house and in the middle of the night he met a ghost. The ghost said, "I have been walking these corridors for 300 years." The man said, "In that case, can you tell me the way to the toilet?"

Why did the ghost go trick-or-treating on the top floor?

He was in high spirits.

What is the favorite game at a ghost's Halloween party?

Hide and Shriek.

Two boys were walking through a churchyard one dark and stormy night. As one stopped to do up his shoelaces they heard an eerie voice coming from behind one of the tombs saying, "Now that I've got you I'm going to eat your legs first, then your arms, then your head and finally I'll gulp down your body." Terrified, the boys ran for the exit but before they could get out of the gate, a figure in black loomed before them.

"I thought I heard someone," said the vicar. "Would you boys like a jelly baby?"

Knock knock.
Who's there?
Augusta.
Augusta who?
August almost felt like winter.

☆ ☆ ☆

Knock knock.
Who's there?
Auntie.
Auntie who?
Auntie glad to see me again?

Knock knock.
Who's there?
Aurora.
Aurora who?
Aurora's just come from a big lion!

☆ ☆ ☆

Knock knock.
Who's there?
Austen.
Austen who?
Austentatiously rich.

☆ ☆ ☆

Knock knock.
Who's there?
Ava.
Ava who?
Ava good mind to leave you.

☆ ☆ ☆

Where do ghoulies go to on the day before a Halloween party?
To the boo-ty parlor.

What's the difference between an adult and a ghost?
One is all grown, the other is all groan.

A ghost came home one night and his wife said "Are you drunk again?" He said, "No of course, not. How dare you!" She replied, "Well you look legless."

Three men are walking along the beach one day when they see a cave. The first man goes in and is just looking at a five-dollar bill on a big rock when a ghostly voice calls out, "I am the ghost of Aunt Mabel and this five dollars stays on the table!" The second man goes in and is reaching for the bill when the same thing happens again. The third man goes in, sees the five dollars and cries out, "I am the ghost of Davie Crockett and this five dollars goes in my pocket!"

Who did the ghost invite to his party?
Anyone he could dig up.

What do you do if you see a skeleton running across the road?
Jump out of your skin and join him.

What's the difference between a
ghost and peanut butter?
A ghost doesn't stick to the roof of
your mouth.

☆   ☆   ☆

What is a skeleton?
Someone who went on a diet and
forgot to say "When."

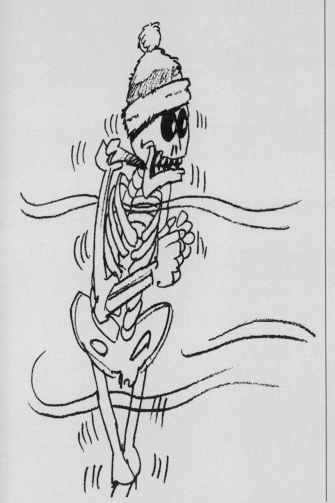

What did the old skeleton complain
of?
Aching bones.

☆   ☆   ☆

Why are skeletons so calm?
Nothing gets under their skin.

☆   ☆   ☆

What do you call a skeleton that's
always telling lies?
A bony phony.

☆   ☆   ☆

What happened to the skeleton that
was attacked by a dog?
It ran off with some bones and left
him without a leg to stand on.

☆   ☆   ☆

What are pupils at ghost schools
called?
Ghoulboys and Ghoulgirls.

☆   ☆   ☆

Knock knock.
Who's there?
Baby.
Baby who?
(sing) "Baby love, my baby love . . ."

Knock knock.
Who's there?
Baby Owl.
Baby Owl who?
Baby Owl see you later, baby not.

Knock knock.
Who's there?
Bach.
Bach who?
Bach to work.

Knock knock.
Who's there?
Bacon.
Bacon who?
Bacon a cake in the oven.

Knock knock.
Who's there?
Barbara.
Barbara who?
(sing) "Barbara black sheep, have
    you any wool?"

A ghost was out haunting one night and met a fairy fluttering through the forest. "Hello," said the ghost. "I've never met a fairy before. What's your name?"

" Nuff," said the fairy.

"That's a very odd name," said the ghost.

"No, it's not," said the fairy, offended. "Haven't you heard of Fairy Nuff?"

Did you hear about the competition to find the laziest spook in the world? All the competitors were lined up on stage. "I've got a really nice, easy job for the laziest person here," said the organizer. "Will the laziest spook raise his hand?" All the spooks put up their hands – except one.

"Why didn't you raise your hand?" asked the presenter.

"Too much trouble," yawned the spook.

What do you call a ghost who only haunts the Town Hall?
The nightmayor.

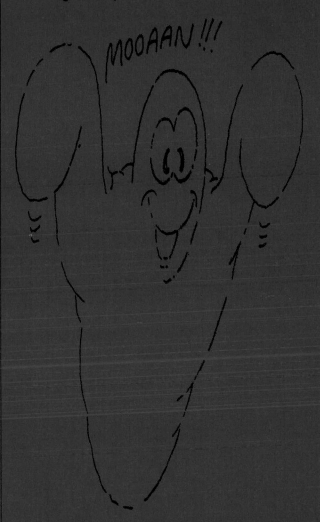

How do you get a ghost to lie perfectly flat?
You use a spirit level.

What happened when the ghostly cows got out of their field?
There was udder chaos.

What did the stupid ghost call his pet tiger?
Spot.

Monster: Stick 'em down.
Ghost: Don't you mean, stick 'em up?
Monster: No wonder I'm not making much money in this business.

☆　☆　☆

Monster: I've got to walk 25 miles home.
Ghost: Why don't you take a train?
Monster: I did once, but my mother made me give it back.

☆　☆　☆

Why don't ghosts make good magicians?
You can see right through their tricks.

Ghost: Are you coming to my party?
Spook: Where is it?
Ghost: In the morgue – you know what they say, the morgue the merrier.

Who wrote Count Dracula's life story?
The ghost writer.

Knock knock.
Who's there?
Bat.
Bat who?
Bat you'll never guess!

☆　☆　☆

Knock knock.
Who's there?
Bea.
Bea who?
Bea love and open the door.

☆　☆　☆

Knock knock.
Who's there?
Bean.
Bean who?
Bean anywhere nice for your
　　vacation?

☆　☆　☆

Knock knock.
Who's there?
Becca.
Becca who?
Becca the net.

☆　☆　☆

Knock knock.
Who's there?
Becker.
Becker who?
Becker the devil you know.

☆　☆　☆

Did you hear about the lady ghoul who went to buy a dress in the Phantom Fashion boutique?
"I'd like to try on that shroud in the window," she told the ghoul in charge.
"Yes, madam," said the ghoul, "but wouldn't you prefer to use the changing room instead?"

Where do ghouls go to study?
Ghoullege.

What do ghosts do at 11 a.m.?
Take a coffin break.

☆　☆　☆

Witch: Try some of my sponge cake.
Wizard: It's a bit tough.
Witch: That's strange. I only bought the sponge from the drugstore this morning.

☆　☆　☆

Spook: Should you eat spiders and slugs and zombie slime on an empty stomach?
Witch: No, you should eat them on a plate.

Witch: I've never been so insulted in my life! I went to a Halloween party, and at midnight they asked me to take my mask off.
Spook: Why are you so angry?
Witch: I wasn't wearing a mask.

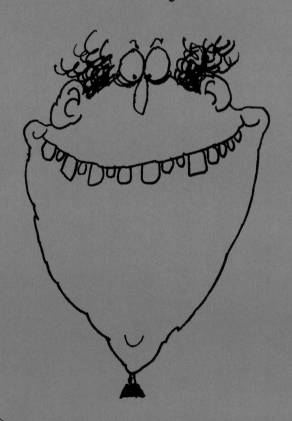

Ghost: I've been invited to an avoidance.
Monster: An avoidance? What's that?
Ghost: It's a dance for people who hate each other.

What does Dracula say to his victims?
It's been nice gnawing you.

What is even more invisible than the invisible ghost?
His shadow.

A flute player was walking home late one night from a concert. He took a short cut through the local woods, and he hadn't gone far before he bumped into a ghost and then a vampire. Pulling out his flute he began to play a lovely trilling melody – the ghost and the vampire stood entranced. Soon the musician was surrounded by a crowd of phantoms, monsters, goblins, cannibals and witches, all listening to the music. Then up bounded a werewolf. "Yum! Yum!" he growled, and gobbled up the flute player.
"Why did you do that?" complained the others. "We were enjoying it."
"Eh, what was that?" said the deaf werewolf.

Knock knock.
Who's there?
Ben and Anna.
Ben and Anna who?
Ben and Anna split.

Knock knock.
Who's there?
Ben Hur.
Ben Hur who?
Ben Hur an hour – let me in!

Knock knock.
Who's there?
Belle.
Belle who?
Belle-t up and open the door.

Knock knock.
Who's there?
Benin.
Benin who?
Benin hell.

Knock knock.
Who's there?
Ben.
Ben who?
Ben down and tie your shoelaces.

Why did the ghost's pants fall down?
Because they had no visible means of
support.

Why was the ghost arrested?
He didn't have a haunting license.

Where do witches' frogs sit?
On toadstools.

Did you hear about the spook who
went on a high-fiber diet?
He had beans on ghost twice a day.

What do you call two witches who
share a broom?
Broom mates.

First Ghost: I saw "The Phantom of
the Opera" last night, on television.
Second Ghost: Was it frightening?
First Ghost: Yes, it half scared the
life into me!

Did you hear about the little spook
who couldn't sleep at night because
his brother kept telling him human
stories?

What's the best way of avoiding infection from biting ghosts?
Don't bite any ghosts.

What did one ghost say to another?
I'm sorry, but I just don't believe in people.

What is a ghost's favorite dessert?
Boo-berry pie with I-scream.

Why are ghosts invisible?
They wear see-through clothes.

First Ghost: I find haunting castles really boring these days.
Second Ghost: I know what you mean. I just don't seem to be able to put any life into it.

☆   ☆   ☆

What do ghosts like about riding horses?
Ghoulloping.

☆   ☆   ☆

What is a ghost's favorite Wild West town?
Tombstone.

☆   ☆   ☆

Why did the ghosts hold a seance?
To try to contact the living.

Knock knock.
Who's there?
Bert.
Bert who?
Bert the cakes.

Knock knock.
Who's there?
Bertha.
Bertha who?
Bertha day boy.

Knock knock.
Who's there?
Beth.
Beth who?
Beth foot forward.

Knock knock.
Who's there?
Bethany.
Bethany who?
Bethany good shows recently?

Knock knock.
Who's there?
Bette.
Bette who?
Bette of roses.

Which weight do ghosts box at?
Phantom weight.

☆   ☆   ☆

First Ghoulish Fiend: I had a nice man to dinner last night.
Second Ghoulish Fiend: So you enjoyed having him?
First Ghoulish Fiend: Oh, yes, he was delicious.

What does a Native American ghost sleep in?
A creepy teepee.

☆   ☆   ☆

What do vampires sing on New Year's Eve?
Auld Fang Syne.

☆   ☆   ☆

What is the American national day for vampires?
Fangsgiving Day.

☆   ☆   ☆

Why did Frankenstein's monster squeeze his girlfriend to death?
He had a crush on her.

☆   ☆   ☆

Boss: Why did you sack your secretary?
Employee: Sickness.
Boss: You mean you sacked her because she was sick?
Employee : No, because the sight of her made me sick.

Suresh: Whatever will Clive do when he leaves school? I can't see him being bright enough to get a job.
Sandra: He could always be a ventriloquist's dummy.

Why did the teacher decide to become an electrician?
To get a bit of light relief.

Did you hear about the dentist who became a brain surgeon?
His drill slipped.

How can you tell if you are looking at a police glow-worm?
He has a blue light.

What do you call a snake that works for the government?
A civil serpent.

Knock knock.
Who's there?
Bettina.
Bettina who?
Bettina minute you'll go to sleep.

Knock knock.
Who's there?
Betty.
Betty who?
Betty earns a lot of money.

Knock knock.
Who's there?
Bhuto.
Bhuto who?
Bhuton the other foot.

Knock knock.
Who's there?
Bill.
Bill who?
Bill of rights.

Knock knock.
Who's there?
B4.
B4 who?
B4 I freeze to death, please open
    this door.

Did you hear about the sailor who was discharged from the submarine service?
He was caught sleeping with the windows open.

What do cannibal secretaries do with leftover fingernails?
They file them.

Was the carpenter's son a chip off the old block?

How does a witch doctor ask a girl to dance?
"Voodoo like to dance with me?"

What happened to the entertainer who did a show for an audience of cannibals?
He went down really well.

Why did Dracula go to the dentist?
He had fang decay.
Why did he have fang decay?
He was always eating fangcy cakes.

Which wizard never goes to the barber?
Hairy Potter.

Why did the vampire give up acting?
He couldn't find a part he could get his teeth into.

What does the mailman take to vampires?
Fang mail.

How can you tell you are talking to an undertaker?
By his grave manner.

What do you have to take to become a coroner?
A stiff exam.

Why was the actor pleased to be on the gallows?
Because at last he was in the noose.

What do witches take to the beach?
Suntan potion.

Surveyor: This house is a ruin. I wonder what stops it from falling down.
Owner: I think the woodworm are holding hands.

Did you hear about the man who left employment at the morgue?
It was a dead-end job.

Knock knock.
Who's there?
Blood.
Blood who?
Blood brothers.

Knock knock.
Who's there?
Blue.
Blue who?
Blue away with the wind.

Knock knock.
Who's there?
Blur.
Blur who?
Blur! It's cold out here.

Knock knock.
Who's there?
Bobby.
Bobby who?
Bobbyn up and down like this.

Knock knock.
Who's there?
Bolton.
Bolton who?
Bolton braces.

Did you hear about the comedian who entertained at a werewolves' party? He had them howling in the aisles.

An idiotic laborer was told by an equally idiotic foreman to dig a hole in the road. "And what shall I do with the earth, sir?" asked the laborer. "Don't be daft, man," replied the foreman. "Just dig another hole and bury it."

Did you hear about the man who set up a flea circus? He started it from scratch.

What do you get if you cross an orange with a comedian? Peels of laughter.

A reporter was captured by some cannibals in the jungle and taken back to the camp where he was prepared for the chief's supper. "What do you do in England?" asked the cook as he was about to light the fire. "I was an editor," replied the journalist. "You'll soon be editor-in-chief" said the cook.

A gymnast who came from Quebec wrapped both legs around his neck. But, sad, he forgot how to untie the knot, and now he's a highly strung wreck.

A man who tests people's eyes is called an optimist.

What has eight legs and likes living in trees?
Four anti-road protesters.

A stupid glazier was examining a broken window. He looked at it for a while and then said: "It's worse than I thought. It's broken on both sides."

"You should get a job in the meteorology office."
"Why?"
"Because you're an expert on wind."

What do a vulture, a pelican and a taxman have in common?
Big bills!

Client: How can I make my money go further?
Financial Adviser: Mail it abroad.

What do a vulture, a pelican and a taxman have in common?

The plumber was working in a house when the lady of the house said to him. "Will it be all right if I have a bath while you're having your lunch?"
"It's OK with me lady," said the plumber, "as long as you don't splash my sandwiches."

Knock knock.
Who's there?
Bones.
Bones who?
Bones upon a time . . .

Knock knock.
Who's there?
Boo.
Boo who?
Oh please don't cry!

Knock knock.
Who's there?
Borg.
Borg who?
Borg standard.

Knock knock.
Who's there?
Bosnia.
Bosnia who?
Bosnia bell here earlier?

Knock knock.
Who's there?
Bowl.
Bowl who?
Bowl me over.

Why did the stupid sailor grab a bar of soap when his ship sank?
He thought he could wash himself ashore.

What's the difference between a bus driver and a cold in the head?
A bus driver knows the stops, and a cold in the head stops the nose.

What did one magician say to another?
Who was that girl I sawed you with last night?

When you leave school, you should become a bone specialist.
You've certainly got the head for it.

How did the man feel when he got a big bill from the electricity company?
A bit shocked.

At three o'clock one morning a veterinarian was woken from a deep sleep by the ringing of his telephone. He staggered downstairs and answered the phone.
"I'm sorry if I woke you," said a voice at the other end of the line.
"That's all right," said the veterinarian, "I had to get up to answer the telephone anyway."

Why was the cleaner unhappy with his job?
Because he believed that grime didn't pay.

Why did the skeleton go to the disco?
He heard it was a hip joint.

First Undertaker: I've just been given the sack.
Second Undertaker: Why?
First Undertaker: I buried someone in the wrong place.
Second Undertaker: That was a grave mistake.

What sort of fish performs operations?
A sturgeon.

How did the baker get an electric shock?
He stood on a bun and a current ran up his leg.

What do traffic wardens like for tea?
Traffic jam sandwiches.

What happens if you tell a psychiatrist you are schizophrenic?
He charges you double.

Knock knock.
Who's there?
Boyzone.
Boyzone who?
Boyzone adventures.

Knock knock.
Who's there?
Brad.
Brad who?
Brad to meet ya!

Knock knock.
Who's there?
Brent.
Brent who?
Brent out of shape.

Knock knock.
Who's there?
Brendan.
Brendan who?
Brendan an ear to what
    I have to say.

Knock knock.
Who's there?
Brian.
Brian who?
Brian drain!

Why do barbers make good drivers?
Because they know all the short cuts.

Did you hear that in the recent gales the fence blew down around the Pink and Pimply Nudist Camp?
A group of builders is looking into it.

What do you get if you cross a caretaker with a monk who smokes large cigars?
A caretaker with a bad habit.

What kind of jokes does a chiropodist like?
Corny jokes.

☆　☆　☆

Why is a caretaker nothing like Robinson Crusoe?
Because Robinson Crusoe got all his work done by Friday.

An extremely tall man with round shoulders, very long arms and one leg six inches shorter than the other went to see a tailor. "I'd like to see a suit that will fit me," he told the tailor. "So would I, sir," the tailor sympathized. "So would I."

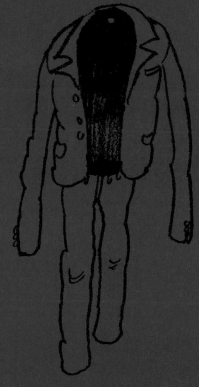

Teacher: And why would you like to be a teacher, Clarence?
Clarence: Because I wouldn't have to learn anything, Sir. I'd know everything by then.

As the judge said to the dentist: Do you swear to pull the tooth, the whole tooth, and nothing but the tooth?

Teacher: Who can tell me what an archeologist is?
Tracey: It's someone whose career is in ruins.

☆   ☆   ☆

Why did the undertaker chop all his corpses into little bits?
Because he liked them to rest in pieces.

☆   ☆   ☆

What's the definition of a good actor?
Somebody who tries hard to be everybody but himself.

☆   ☆   ☆

Do undertakers enjoy their job?
Of corpse they do.

☆   ☆   ☆

Why did the composer spend all his time in bed?
He wrote sheet music.

☆   ☆   ☆

Who has the most dangerous job in Transylvania?
Dracula's dentist.

☆   ☆   ☆

Why did the doughnut maker retire?
He was fed up with the hole business.

☆   ☆   ☆

Knock knock.
Who's there?
Bruno.
Bruno who?
Bruno more tea for me.

Knock knock.
Who's there?
Bug.
Bug who?
Bug Rogers.

Knock knock.
Who's there?
Bug.
Bug who?
Bugsy Malone.

Knock knock.
Who's there?
Brook.
Brook who?
Brooklyn Bridge.

Knock knock.
Who's there?
Brother.
Brother who?
Brotheration! I've forgotten my own
    name!

A man went into a tailor's shop and saw a man hanging by one arm from the center of the ceiling. "What's he doing there?" he asked the tailor. "Oh, pay no attention," said the tailor, "he thinks he's a light bulb." "Well, why don't you tell him he isn't?" asked the startled customer. "What," replied the tailor, "and work in the dark?"

☆ ☆ ☆

"Why did you leave your last job?"
"Something the boss said."
"Was he abusive?"
"Not exactly."
"What did he say, then?"
"You're fired!"

"Good morning, sir. I'm applying for the job as handyman."
"I see. Well, are you handy?"
"Couldn't be more so. I only live next door."

☆ ☆ ☆

The new office boy came into his boss's office and said, "I think you're wanted on the phone, sir."
"What d'you mean, you think?" demanded the boss.
"Well, sir, the phone rang, I answered it and a voice said, 'Is that you, you old fool?'"

☆ ☆ ☆

An apprentice blacksmith was told by his master to make a hammer. The lad had not the slightest idea how to begin, so he thought he'd be crafty and nip out and buy one. He duly showed the new hammer to his master who said, "That's excellent boy! Now make 50 more just like it."

☆ ☆ ☆

Why do you want to work in a bank?
Well, I'm told there's money in it.

"Very well, my boy," said the manager, "I'll take you on. I take it you're not afraid of early hours?"
"Oh no, sir," said the teenage applicant, "you can't close too early for me!"

"Mossop! Why are you late this morning?"
"I got married, sir."
"Very well, but see that it doesn't happen again."

"You play fair with me and I'll play fair with you," said the boss to the new worker. "Just remember: you can't do too much for a good employer."
"Don't worry, I won't."

"Come on, slowpoke," said the foreman to a tardy workman, "the hooter's gone."
"Don't look at me, sir. I didn't take it!"

The butcher's boy had been dismissed for insolence, and vowed vengeance on his ex-employer. The following Saturday morning, when the shop was packed with people buying their weekend joints, he marched in, elbowed his way to the counter and slapped down one very, very dead cat. "There you are, sir!" he called out cheerily. "That makes up the dozen you ordered."

Knock knock.
Who's there?
Butcher.
Butcher who?
Butcher left leg in, your left leg out . . .

Knock knock.
Who's there?
Butter.
Butter who?
Butter wrap up – it's cold out here.

Knock knock.
Who's there?
Butter.
Butter who?
Butter hurry up – I need the toilet now!

Knock knock.
Who's there?
Byron.
Byron who?
Byron new suit.

Knock knock.
Who's there?
Buster.
Buster who?
Buster tyre, can I use your phone?

"I just want you to remember one thing, Boyce," said the managing director to the new sales manager. "If at first you don't succeed – you're fired!"

The young lad had applied for a job, and was asked his full name.
"Aloysius Montmorency Geoghan," he replied.
"How do you spell that?" asked the manager.
"Er – sir – er – can't you just put it down without spelling it?"

"I was a waiter at the Hotel Splendiferous for three months, but I had to leave on account of the head waiter's nerves."
"His nerves?"
"He couldn't stand the sound of breaking crockery."

The apprentice electrician was on his first job. "Take hold of those two wires, Alex," said his master, "and rub them together." Alex did as he was bid, and his master said, "Do you feel anything?"
"No," said Alex.
"That's good – so don't touch those other two wires, they must be the live ones!"

"I'm the boss and you're nothing!"
"What are you?"
"Nothing."
"And what am I?"
"Boss over nothing."
"Pshaw! You're next to an idiot."
"Very well, I'll move."

"Why did you leave your last employment?"

"The boss accused me of stealing a five-dollar bill."

"But why didn't you make him prove it?"

"He did."

"You're late for work again, Lamport!"

"Yes, I'm sorry, sir. I overslept."

"I thought I told you to get an alarm clock."

"I did, sir, but there are nine of us in our family."

"What's that got to do with it?"

"The alarm was only set for eight!"

"Did your previous employer give you a reference?"

"Yes, but I left it at home."

"What does it say?"

"Er, well, it says I was one of the best employees that he had ever turned out . . ."

"I thought, Jessop, that you wanted yesterday afternoon off because you were seeing your dentist?"

"That's right, sir."

"So how come I saw you and a friend coming out of the football ground at the end of a game?"

"That was my dentist."

"I need a smart boy," said the boss to the young applicant. "Someone quick to take notice."

"Oh, I can do that, sir. I had it twice last week."

Knock knock.
Who's there?
Cain.
Cain who?
Cain tell you.

☆   ☆   ☆

Knock knock.
Who's there?
Caitlin.
Caitlin who?
Caitlin you my dress tonight – I'm
    wearing it.

☆   ☆   ☆

Knock knock.
Who's there?
Caesar.
Caesar who?
Caesar arm to stop her getting
    away.

☆   ☆   ☆

Knock knock.
Who's there?
Callum.
Callum who?
Callum all back.

☆   ☆   ☆

Knock knock.
Who's there?
Caesar.
Caesar who?
Caesar jolly good fellow.

☆   ☆   ☆

What did the gardener say when he saw his none-too-bright assistant laying the lawn at a new house? "Green on top!"

The manager of a store observed one of his customers in a furious argument with a junior clerk. As he hurried over, the customer finally yelled, " . . . and I shall never come into this place again!", then stalked out, slamming the door behind him. "Hicks," said the manager severely, "how many more times must I tell you that the customer is always right." "As you wish sir," said the junior. "He was saying you were a lop-eared, bald-headed, brainless twit!"

"If you're going to work here, young man," said the boss, "one thing you must learn is that we are very keen on cleanliness in this firm. Did you wipe your feet on the mat as you came in?"
"Oh, yes sir."
"And another thing, we are very keen on truthfulness. There is no mat."

"Don't you like being a telegraph linesman?"
"No, it's driving me up the pole."

☆   ☆   ☆

Why did the lazy man get a job in a bakery?
Because he wanted a good loaf.

☆   ☆   ☆

What training do you need to be a garbage collector?
None, you pick it up as you go along.

Son: I want to drive a bus when I grow up.
Father: I won't stand in your way.

What happens when plumbers die?
They go down the drain.

What do you call a gooseberry who insults a farmer?
Fresh fruit.

Peter: My brother wants to work badly.
Anita: As I remember, he usually does.

A man coughed violently, and his false teeth shot across the room and smashed against the wall. "Oh dear," he said, "whatever shall I do? I can't afford a new set."
"Don't worry," said his friend. "I'll get a pair from my brother for you."
The next day the friend came back with the teeth, which fitted perfectly. "This is wonderful," said the man. "Your brother must be a very good dentist."
"Oh, he's not a dentist," replied the friend, "he's an undertaker."

☆ ☆ ☆

Penny: No one could call your dad a quitter.
Kenny: No, he's been sacked from every job he's ever had.

☆ ☆ ☆

What should you do if your plumb falls ill?
Call the plumber.

Knock knock.
Who's there?
Carl.
Carl who?
Carl you see?

Knock knock.
Who's there?
Carlene.
Carlene who?
Carlene against that wall!

Knock knock.
Who's there?
Carlo.
Carlo who?
Carload of junk.

Knock knock.
Who's there?
Carmen.
Carmen who?
Carmen like best is a Ferrari.

Knock knock.
Who's there?
Carol.
Carol who?
Carol go if you switch
   the ignition on.

What did the dentist say when his wife baked an apple pie?
"Can I do the filling?"

What sort of vegetables do plumbers fix?
Leeks.

What happened to the potato that refused to work?
It was sacked.

They say he works eight hours and sleeps eight hours. Problem is, they're the same eight hours.

Boss: Are you willing to do an honest day's work?
Secretary: Yes, as long as you give me an honest week's pay for it.

"My brother took an aptitude test to discover what he was best suited for."

"And what did it reveal?"
"That he was best suited for retirement."

What happened to the plastic surgeon who stood too close to the fire?
He melted.

Why did they give the mailman the sack?
To put his letters in.

ADVERTISEMENT: Secretary required. Computer skills essential but not compulsory.

"They say the only exercise he gets is watching old horror movies on the TV."
"How does that give him exercise?"
"They make his flesh creep."

Why did the farmer run a steamroller over his potato patch?
Because he wanted mashed potatoes.

Where do frogs go when they have bad eyesight?
To a hoptometrist.

Susie: Is it true that your dad is a miracle worker?
Sally: Yes. It's a miracle when he works.

"He started at the bottom."
"Yes, and enjoyed it so much he's been there ever since."

"I hear they call him Caterpillar."
"Why's that?"
"He got where he is by crawling."

Knock knock.
Who's there?
Cattle.
Cattle who?
Cattle purr if you stroke it.

Knock knock.
Who's there?
Cecile.
Cecile who?
Cecile th-the w-windows. Th-there's
  a m-monster out there.

Knock knock.
Who's there?
Cecile.
Cecile who?
Cecile the envelope.

Knock knock.
Who's there?
Celeste.
Celeste who?
Celeste time I come calling.

Knock knock.
Who's there?
Cello.
Cello who?
Cello, how are you?

First Boss: At least Cynthia's dependable.
Second Boss: Yes, you can usually depend upon her to do the wrong thing.

Mother: Do you think Sally should take up the piano as a career?
Music Teacher: No, I think she should put down the lid as a favor.

WANTED: Male waitress.

A lady vicar is called a vixen.

"He'd never make a photographer."
"Why not?"
"Every time he's in the darkroom trouble develops."

"They say he wanted to be a doctor badly."
"Well, he's certainly a bad doctor."

Did you hear about the flower arranger's children?
One was a budding genius, the other was a blooming idiot!

"His father's an optometrist."
"Is that why he makes such a spectacle of himself?"

Keith: I'm looking for a job. What shall I do?
Kevin: Apply at the cobbler's, I've heard he's looking for heels.

"You'd make a good model."
"Because of my looks?"
"No, because you're such a poser."

Jerry: I could be a famous brain surgeon if I had a mind to.
Terry: Yes that's the problem, isn't it? You don't have a mind.

Lady of the Manor: And breakfast is at 7.30 sharp.
New Maid: OK, but if I'm not up, you can start without me.

Knock knock.
Who's there?
Che.
Che who?
Che what you're made of.

Knock knock.
Who's there?
Cheese.
Cheese who?
Cheese a jolly good fellow.

Knock knock.
Who's there?
Cher.
Cher who?
Cher and share alike!

Knock knock.
Who's there?
Chest.
Chest who?
Chestnuts for sale!

Knock knock.
Who's there?
Chester.
Chester who?
Chester drawers.

Boss: That new clerk is useless.
Personnel Manager: Oh dear.
Boss: Yes, he's only been here a week and already he's a month behind in his work!

Angry Voice on the Phone: Doesn't your company ever answer letters?
Stupid Secretary: Oh dear, haven't you had our letter, yet? I'm about to send it to you.

Surgeon: I think you've just cut an artery.
Medical Student: Oh dear, aorta know better.

"Is it possible to tell when a politician is lying?"
"Oh yes, I can always tell."
"How?"
"Their lips move."

Barber: Have you been here before?
Customer: Yes.
Barber: I'm afraid I don't remember your face.
Customer: Well, it's all healed up now.

The teacher was trying to instill into her class the virtues of hard work. "Take," she said, "the example of the ant. It works and works all the time. And what is the result of all this work?"
Clever Clogs Charlie: "Someone treads on it, Miss."

Kelly: Is God a doctor, Miss?
Teacher: In some ways, Kelly. Why do you ask?
Kelly: Because the Bible says that the Lord gave the tablets to Moses.

What school subject are snakes best at?
Hiss-tory.

What is the first thing that bats learn at school?
The alphabat.

☆ ☆ ☆

What's the difference between school dinners and a pile of slugs?
School dinners come on a plate.

☆ ☆ ☆

Teacher: Who can tell me what "dogma" means?
Cheeky Charlie: It's a lady dog that's had puppies, Sir.

What is the difference between a poisonous snake and a principal?
You can make a pet out of the snake.

How did the teacher knit a suit of armor?
She used steel wool.

Knock knock.
Who's there?
Chris.
Chris who?
Christmas stocking.

Knock knock.
Who's there?
Chrome.
Chrome who?
Chromosome.

Knock knock.
Who's there?
Chrysalis.
Chrysalis who?
Chrysalis the cake for you.

Knock knock.
Who's there?
Chocs.
Chocs who?
Chocs away!

Knock knock.
Who's there?
Chopin.
Chopin who?
Chopin the department store.

My sister's singing's very educational. Every time she starts I shut myself up in my room with my homework.

Why was the big, hairy, two-headed monster top of the class at school? Because two heads are better than one.

What's the favorite subject of young witches at school?
Spelling.

☆   ☆   ☆

What happened to the naughty little witch at school?
She was ex-spelled.

☆   ☆   ☆

What do little witches like to play at school?
Bat's cradle.

☆   ☆   ☆

"Ann," said the dancing mistress. "There are two things stopping you becoming the world's greatest ballerina."
"What are they, Miss?" asked Ann.
"Your feet."

Alex's class went on a nature study ramble. "What do you call a thing with ten legs, red spots and great big jaws, Sir?" asked Alex.
"I've no idea, why do you ask?" replied the teacher.
"Because one just crawled up your trouser leg."

Why didn't the skeleton want to go to school?
Because his heart wasn't in it.

What do you call an ant who honestly hates school?
A tru-ant.

Young Horace was being taught how to box, but so far hadn't landed a single blow on his opponent.
"Don't worry, lad," said his teacher, "keep swinging, the draft might give him a cold."

Teacher: What did you get for Christmas, Jimmy?
Jimmy: A mouth organ. It's the best present I ever got.
Teacher: Why?
Jimmy: My mom gives me ten cents a week not to blow it.

First Monster: What is that son of yours doing these days?
Second Monster: He's at medical school.
First Monster: Oh, what's he studying?
Second Monster: Nothing, they're studying him.

"Mary," said her teacher. "You can't bring that lamb into school. What about the smell?"
"Oh, that's all right, Miss," said Mary. "It'll soon get used to it."

Knock knock.
Who's there?
Clark.
Clark who?
Clark your car out here.

☆   ☆   ☆

Knock knock.
Who's there?
Claudette.
Claudette who?
Claudette a whole cake.

☆   ☆   ☆

Knock knock.
Who's there?
Clay.
Clay who?
Clay on, Sam.

☆   ☆   ☆

Knock knock.
Who's there?
Cliff.
Cliff who?
Cliff hanger.

☆   ☆   ☆

Knock knock.
Who's there?
Clinton.
Clinton who?
Clinton your eye.

Principal: Teachers like Mr Flopple don't grow on trees, you know.
Neil, under his breath: No, they swing from them.

Did you hear about the posh school where all the pupils smelled?
It was for filthy rich kids only.

"I told you to draw a picture of a cow eating grass," said the art master. "Why have you handed in a blank sheet of paper?"
"Because the cow ate all the grass, that's why there's no grass."
"But what about the cow?"
"There wasn't much point in hanging around when there was nothing to eat, so she went back to the byre."

Why do vampires do well at school?
Because every time they're asked a question they come up with a biting reply.

Teacher: If you saw me standing by a witch, what fruit would it remind you of?
Pupil: A pear.

Coach: How's the new player coming along?
Team Captain: He's trying.
Coach: I've heard he's very trying.

Two girls were having their packed lunch in the school playground. One had an apple and the other said, "Watch out for worms won't you!"
The first one replied "Why should I? They can watch out for themselves."

Be sure that you go straight home.
I can't, I live around the corner!

There once was a schoolboy named Rhett.
Who ate ten chocolate bars for a bet.
When asked, "Are you faint?"
He said, "No I ain't.
But I don't feel like flying a jet."

Two schoolboys were talking about their math lessons. "Why do you suppose we stop the tables at 12?" asked one.
"Oh, don't you know," said the other. "I heard Mom say it was unlucky to have 13 at table."

"Ann, point out Australia for me on the map." Ann went to the front of the class, picked up the pointer and showed the rest of the class where Australia was.
"Well done! Now, Alec! Can you tell us who discovered Australia?"
"Er . . . Ann, Miss?"

☆　☆　☆

Found in the School Library: The Broken Window by Eva Brick

☆　☆　☆

"Lie flat on your backs, class, and circle your feet in the air as if you were riding your bikes," said the PE teacher. "Alec! What are you doing? Move your feet, boy!"
"I'm freewheeling, Sir."

☆　☆　☆

Teacher: Can anyone tell me what a shamrock is?
Jimmy: It's a fake diamond, Miss.

Knock knock.
Who's there?
Closure.
Closure who?
Closure mouth when you're eating!

Knock knock.
Who's there?
Coffin.
Coffin who?
Coffin and spluttering.

Knock knock.
Who's there?
Cohen.
Cohen who?
Cohen your way.

Knock knock.
Who's there?
Cole.
Cole who?
Cole as a cucumber.

Knock knock.
Who's there?
Colin.
Colin who?
Colin and see me next time you're
    passing.

When Dad came home he was astonished to see Alec sitting on a horse, writing something.

"What on earth are you doing there?" he asked.

"Well, teacher told us to write an essay on our favorite animal. That's why I'm here and that's why Susie's sitting in the goldfish bowl!"

"What were you before you came to school, boys and girls?" asked the teacher, hoping that someone would say "Babies." She was disappointed when all the children cried out, "Happy!"

Did you hear about the schoolboy who couldn't get to grips with decimals? He just couldn't see the point.

"Jean, define a baby."

"A soft pink thing that makes a lot of noise at one end and has no sense of responsibility at the other."

"In some countries," said the geography teacher, "men are allowed more than one wife. That's called polygamy. In others, women are allowed more than one husband. That's called polyandry. In this country, men and women are allowed only one married partner. Can anyone tell me what that's called?"

"Monotony, Sir!"

Janet came home from school and asked her mother if the aerosol spray in the kitchen was hair lacquer. "No," said Mom. "It's glue."

"I thought so," said Janet. "I wondered why I couldn't get my beret off today."

"What are the elements, Alec?" asked the science teacher.

"Er . . . earth . . . air . . . fire . . ."

"Well done," said the teacher. "There's one more."

"Er . . . oh yes. Golf."

"Golf!"

"Yes, I heard my mom say that dad's in his element when he plays golf."

☆   ☆   ☆

When Bud, an American boy, visited an English school, the physical education teacher asked Alec to explain the rules of cricket to him.

"Well," said Alec, "there are two sides, one out in the field and one in the pavilion. Each man in the side that's in goes out and when he's out he comes in and the next man goes in until he's out. When they're all out, the side that's been out comes in and the side that's been in goes out and tries to get the players coming in, out. When both sides have been in and out, including the not-outs, that's the end of the game."

"Thanks," said Bud. "I'll stick to baseball."

☆   ☆   ☆

Teacher: Do you have any sisters or brothers?

Millie: No, I'm an only child.

Teacher: Thank goodness for that!

☆   ☆   ☆

Knock knock.
Who's there?
Colin.
Colin who?
Colin all cars . . . Colin all cars . . .

Knock knock.
Who's there?
Colleen.
Colleen who?
Colleen yourself up, you're a mess!

Knock knock.
Who's there?
Collie.
Collie who?
Collie Miss Molly, I don't know.

Knock knock.
Who's there?
Cologne.
Cologne who?
Cologne around the world and meet
     people.

Knock knock.
Who's there?
Congo.
Congo who?
Congo into the woods – it's
     dangerous.

Mr Anderson, the science teacher, was very absent-minded. One day he brought a box into the classroom and said, "I've got a frog and a toad in here. When I get them out we'll look at the differences." He put his hand into the box and pulled out two sandwiches. "Oh dear!" he said. "I could have sworn I'd just had my lunch."

"Why are you crying, Amanda?" asked her teacher.
"Cos Jenny's broken my new doll Miss," she cried.
"How did she do that?"
"I hit her on the head with it."

"That's an excellent essay for someone your age," said the English teacher.
"How about for someone my Mom's age, Miss?"

One day a teacher came into her classroom and found a very rude word chalked on her blackboard. "I'm not going to scold," she said. "We're going to take care of this by the honor system. We'll all close our eyes and I'll count up to 100. When we open our eyes, whoever wrote that will have tiptoed up to the board and erased it." Everyone closed their eyes. 1 . . . 2 . . . 3 . . . pitter pitter . . . 48 . . . 49 . . . 50 . . . squeak, squeak . . . 99, 100. Everyone opened their eyes and there, on the board, was another, even filthier word and above it was chalked, "The phantom writer strikes again."

Confucius he say: If teacher ask you question and you not know answer, mumble.

"I see you've got that new boy down for the game against Brick Street," said the English teacher to the PE master.

"Yes, but I'm not sure what position to play him."

" Well if his football's anything like his English, he's a natural drawback."

What's the longest piece of furniture in the school?
The multiplication table.

"Did you thank Mrs Pillbeam for teaching you today?" Alec's mom asked him when he came home from school.

"No I didn't. Mary in front of me did and Mrs Pillbeam said, 'Don't mention it,' so I didn't."

Little Tommy was the quietest boy in school. He never answered any questions but his homework was always quite excellent. If anyone said anything to him he would simply nod, or shake his head. The staff thought he was shy and decided to do something to give him confidence.
"Tommy," said his teacher. "I've just bet Miss Smith $5 I can get you to say three words. You can have half." Tommy looked at her pityingly and said, "You lose."

How do Religious Education teachers mark exams?
With spirit levels.

Knock knock.
Who's there?
Costas.
Costas who?
Costas a fortune to get here.

Knock knock.
Who's there?
Courtney.
Courtney who?
Courtney robbers lately?

Knock knock.
Who's there?
Carlotta.
Carlotta who?
Carlotta trouble when it breaks
   down.

Knock knock.
Who's there?
Cousin.
Cousin who?
Cousin stead of opening the door
   you're leaving me here.

Knock knock.
Who's there?
Craig.
Craig who?
Craig in the wall.

A very new and very nervous school inspector was being shown round a very rough school. Just as the tour of inspection was coming to an end, the principal asked him if he'd mind saying a few words of advice to a class of unruly 16-year-olds who were going to leave school at the end of term. The principal managed to get the kids to be quiet, introduced them to the inspector and told them that he was going to say a few words to them. The poor man was totally nonplussed by the sight of the unwelcoming faces staring at him, but he took a deep breath and began: "When y-y-y-you were in-in-infants I'm sure you enjoyed your in-in-infancy. As ch-ch-children I'm sure you enjoyed y-y-y-your ch-ch-childhood. I c-c-c-can see that you are enjoying your a-a-a-a-adolescence and I h-h-hope that w-w-when you leave school and become adults, you will enjoy your adultery."

Did you hear what happened when there was an epidemic of laryngitis at school?
The school nurse sent everyone to the croakroom.

Teacher at High-Class School: Now, remember, Samantha, a young lady never crumbles her bread or rolls in her soup.

I enjoy doing my homework
Even at weekends.
But my best friend's just told me
He thinks I'm round the bend.

Thinking he would play a trick on the biology teacher, Alec glued a beetle's head to a caterpillar's body and very carefully attached some butterfly wings, ant's legs and a fly's tail. The teacher was very impressed. "I've never seen anything like this, Alec," he said. "Tell me. Did it hum when you caught it?"

"Why yes, sir. Quite loudly."

"I thought so. It's a humbug."

"How old are you?"

"I'm not old," said Simon. "I'm nearly new."

"Please, Miss!" said a little boy at kindergarten. "We're going to play elephants and circuses, do you want to join in?"

"I'd love to," said the teacher. "What do you want me to do?"

"You can be the lady that feeds us peanuts!"

I smother school dinner with honey.
I've done it all my life.
It makes the food taste funny.
But the peas stay on my knife.

What's the difference between a schoolboy and an angler?
One baits his hooks. The other hates his books.

What do you get if you cross old potatoes with lumpy mince?
School dinners.

Knock knock.
Who's there?
Crock and Dial.
Crock and Dial who?
Crock and Dial Dundee.

Knock knock.
Who's there?
Cuba.
Cuba who?
Cuba wood.

Knock knock.
Who's there?
Curry.
Curry who?
Curry me all the way.

Knock knock.
Who's there?
Cynthia.
Cynthia who?
Cynthia won't listen, I'll keep
   shouting.

Knock knock.
Who's there?
Cyprus.
Cyprus who?
Cyprus the bell?

Knock knock.
Who's there?
Dad.
Dad who?
Dadda! Let's roll out the red carpet!

Knock knock.
Who's there?
Daisy.
Daisy who?
Daisy that you are in, but I don't believe them.

Knock knock.
Who's there?
Dakota.
Dakota who?
Dakota is too small around the neck.

Knock knock.
Who's there?
Dale.
Dale who?
Dale come if you call dem.

Knock knock.
Who's there?
Dana.
Dana who?
Dana you mind.

94

"Your daughter's only five and she can spell her name backwards? Why, that is remarkable." The principal was talking to a parent who was trying to impress her with the child's academic prowess so that she would be accepted into the school.

"Yes, we're very proud of her," said the mother.

"And what is your daughter's name?"

"Anna."

The night school teacher asked one of his pupils when he had last sat an exam. "1945," said the lad.

"Good lord! That's more than 50 years ago."

"No, Sir! An a hour and a half. It's quarter past nine now."

"I'd like you to be very quiet today, boys and girls. I've got a dreadful headache."

"Please, Miss!" said Alec. "Why don't you do what Mom does when she has a headache."

"What's that?"

"She sends us out to play."

"Mommy," sobbed the little girl. "I told teacher that great-great-grandpapa died at Waterloo," and she said, 'Really, which platform?'and everybody giggled."

"Well next time she says that you just tell her that the platform number is irrelevant."

PE mistress: Come on, Sophie. You can run faster than that.

Sophie: I can't, Miss. I'm wearing run-resistant panty hose.

What did the arithmetic book say to the geometry book?
Boy! Do we have our problems!

A warning to any young sinner,
Be you fat or perhaps even thinner.
If you do not repent,
To Hell you'll be sent.
With nothing to eat but school dinner.

Why are American schoolchildren extremely healthy?
Because they have a good constitution.

An English teacher asked her class to write an essay on what they'd do if they had $1,000,000. Alec handed in a blank sheet of paper. "Alec!" yelled the teacher. "You've done nothing. Why?"
"Cos if I had $1,000,000 that's exactly what I would do."

"And what's your name?" the school secretary asked a new boy.
"Butter."
"I hope your first name's not Roland," smirked the secretary.
"No, Miss. It's Brendan."

A little girl was next in line.
"My name's Curtain," she said.
"I hope your first name's not Annette."
"No. It's Velvet."

Knock knock.
Who's there?
Dave.
Dave who?
Dave-andalized our home.

Knock knock.
Who's there?
Dave.
Dave who?
Dave of glory.

Knock knock.
Who's there?
Dawn.
Dawn who?
Dawn do anything I wouldn't do.

☆   ☆   ☆

Knock knock.
Who's there?
Debbie.
Debbie who?
Debbie or not to be.

Knock knock.
Who's there?
Debussy.
Debussy who?
Debussy's never on time!

Knock knock.
Who's there?
Delhi.
Delhi who?
Delhi a joke . . .

Knock knock.
Who's there?
Della.
Della who?
Della tell ya that I love ya?

Knock knock.
Who's there?
Delphine.
Delphine who?
Delphine fine, thanks.

Knock knock.
Who's there?
Delta.
Delta who?
Delta great hand of cards.

Knock knock.
Who's there?
Demi Moore.
Demi Moore who?
Demi Moore than you did last time.

Knock knock.
Who's there?
Derek.
Derek who?
Derek get richer and the poor get
     poorer.

Knock knock.
Who's there?
Desi.
Desi who?
Desi take sugar?

Knock knock.
Who's there?
Devlin.
Devlin who?
Devlin a red dress.

☆   ☆   ☆

Knock knock.
Who's there?
Dewey.
Dewey who?
Dewey stay or do we go now?

☆   ☆   ☆

Knock knock.
Who's there?
Diana.
Diana who?
Diana thirst – a glass of water,
     please.

☆   ☆   ☆

"What's your first name?" the school secretary asked a new boy.

"It's Orson, Miss. I was named after Orson Welles, the movie star."

"Just as well your last name's not Cart. Isn't it?"

"Yes, Miss. It's Trapp."

At the school concert, Wee Willie had volunteered to play his bagpipes. The noise was dreadful, like a choir of cats singing off-key. After he'd blown his way through 'The Flowers of the Forest,' he said, "Is there anything you'd like me to play?"

"Yes!" cried a voice from the back of the hall. "Dominoes!"

"Dad," said Billy to his father who was a bank robber, "I need $50 for the school trip tomorrow."

"OK, son," said his dad, "I'll get you the cash when the bank closes."

"I'm very sad to announce this morning, boys and girls, that Miss Jones has decided to retire," said the principal at morning assembly. "Now we will all stand and sing this morning's hymn . . . 'Now Thank We All Our God'."

Did you hear about the schoolboy who was studying Greek mythology? When the teacher asked him to name something that was half-man and half-beast he replied Buffalo Bill.

"Why don't you like this country?" the teacher asked a Californian boy who had come to an English school.

"It's the weather," drawled Bud. "I'm not used to the rain. At home we have 365 days of sunshine every year – at least."

Svenda Norselander, a girl from Lapland, came to our school for a term.

"We have geography lessons first," said the teacher.

"I am not knowing the geography," said Svenda.

"How about history?"

"I am not knowing the history."

"Science?"

"What is this science?"

"Chemistry? Physics? Biology?"

"I know not what these things are."

"What do you know?" asked the teacher, trying to keep her temper.

"I am knowing how to breed reindeer."

That was the last straw. "We don't need to breed rain here!" cried the teacher. "We have enough already. And don't be so familiar with me on your first day."

Rich Boy to Dinner Lady: This bread's horrible. Why can't you make your own bread like the servants do at home?

Dinner Lady: Because we don't have the kind of dough that your father makes!

Principal: If you liked your pupils you'd take them to the zoo.

Teacher: Oh, I know some of them are like animals, but they can't be that bad, surely.

Knock knock.
Who's there?
Diaz.
Diaz who?
Diaz of our lives.

Knock knock.
Who's there?
Dickon.
Dickon who?
Dickon the right answer.

Knock knock.
Who's there?
Diego.
Diego who?
Diego before de "B."

Knock knock.
Who's there?
Diesel.
Diesel who?
Diesel make you feel better.

☆   ☆   ☆

Knock knock.
Who's there?
Dimaggio.
Dimaggio who?
Dimaggio yourself on a deserted
    island . . .

"Who was Captain Kidd?" asked the history teacher.

"He was a contortionist."

"What makes you think that, Alec?"

"Well it says in the history book that he spent a lot of time sitting on his chest."

When the school was broken into, the thieves took absolutely everything – desks, books, blackboards, everything apart from the soap in the lavatories and all the towels.

The police are looking for a pair of dirty criminals.

Something to say to a dinner lady: "Excuse me, are these sesame seeds or have you just sneezed?"

The principal was very proud of his school's academic record. "It is very impressive," said one parent who was considering sending his son there. "How do you maintain such high standards?"

"Simple," said the principal. "The school motto says it all."

"What's that?" asked the parent.

"If at first you don't succeed, you're expelled."

Knock, knock.

Who's there?

Canoe.

Canoe who?

Canoe help me with my homework, please, Dad. I'm stuck.

What's the difference between a boring teacher and a boring book? You can shut the book up.

Two parents were waiting at the school gate. "Look at that teacher," said one to the other. "It's disgraceful. Jeans, a rugby shirt, trainers, cropped blue hair. You'd never think she was a teacher, would you?"
"Well I would actually. That's my child. We're meeting here to go shopping together."
"Oh I'm sorry. I didn't realize you were her mother."
"I'm not. I'm her father actually! And she's my son!"

Did you hear about the brilliant geography master?
He had abroad knowledge of his subject.

Typing Teacher: Bob! Your work has certainly improved. There are only ten mistakes here.
Bob: Oh good, Miss.
Teacher: Now let's look at the second line, shall we?

☆   ☆   ☆

Why did the flea fail his exams?
He wasn't up to scratch.

☆   ☆   ☆

What's the most important thing to remember in Chemistry?
Never lick the spoon.

Knock knock.
Who's there?
Doctor.
Doctor Who?
That's right – where's my Tardis?

Knock knock.
Who's there?
Dolly.
Dolly who?
Dolly't us in, we're cold!

Knock knock.
Who's there?
Dome.
Dome who?
Dome you recognize my voice?

Knock knock.
Who's there?
Don.
Don who?
Don take me for granted.

Knock knock.
Who's there?
Donna.
Donna who?
Donna you know? Isa Luigi.

Teacher: If you add 20,567 to 23,678 and then divide by 92 what do you get?

Jim: The wrong answer.

Two little girls at a very posh school were talking to each other. "I told the chauffeur to take his peaked cap off in case the other girls here thought I was a snob," said the first.

"How strange," said the second. "I told mine to keep his on in case anyone thought he was my father."

The principal was interviewing a new teacher. "You'll get $20,000 to start, with $25,000 after six months."

"Oh!" said the teacher. "I'll come back in six months then."

"I asked you to draw a pony and trap," said the art master. "You've only drawn the pony. Why?"

"Well, Sir. I thought the pony would draw the trap."

At a very upper-class school the girls were discussing their family pets.

"We've got a beautiful spaniel at our place," said one girl.

"Does it have a pedigree?" asked another.

"It does on its mother's side. And its father comes from a very good neighborhood."

Teacher: Who can tell me what geese eat?

Paul: Er, gooseberries, Sir?

"What's your father's occupation?" asked the school secretary on the first day of the new term.

"He's a conjurer, Miss," said the new boy.

"How interesting. What's his favorite trick?"

"He saws people in half."

"Golly! Now next question. Any brothers and sisters?"

"One half-brother and two half-sisters."

The music teacher could not control her class. A deafening noise always came from her room. One day when it was worse than usual the English mistress could bear it no longer. She ran into the music room, where she found the music teacher sitting at her piano and the boys and girls raising Cain. "Do you know my pupils can't concentrate for the din in here?" the English teacher said.

"No!" said the music teacher. "But if you hum it I'll try and follow."

"Alec won't be at school today," said his mother on the telephone. "He's broken an arm."

"Well tell him we hope he gets better soon."

"Oh he's fine now," said the mother. "It was my arm he broke."

Knock knock.
Who's there?
Douglas.
Douglas who?
Douglas is broken.

Knock knock.
Who's there?
Dozen.
Dozen who?
Dozen anyone know my name?

Knock knock.
Who's there?
Drum.
Drum who?
Drum as fast as you can.

Knock knock.
Who's there?
Duane.
Duane who?
Duane gonna get away with dis!

Knock knock.
Who's there?
Dublin.
Dublin who?
Dublin up with laughter.

"Please, Sir. There's something wrong with my stomach."
"Well button up your jacket and no one will notice."

The school teacher was furious when Alec knocked him down with his new bicycle in the playground. "Don't you know how to ride that yet?" he roared.
"Oh yes!" shouted Alec over his shoulder. "It's the bell I can't work yet."

On the first day at school the children were sizing each other up and boasting, trying to make good impressions on each other. "I come from a one-parent family," said one little girl proudly.
"That's nothing. Both my parents remarried after they got divorced. I come from a four-parent family."

Billy's mother was called into the school one day by the principal. "We're very worried about Billy," he said. "He goes round all day 'cluck, cluck, clucking.'"
"That's right," said Billy's mother. "He thinks he's a chicken."
"Haven't you taken him to a psychiatrist?"
"Well we would but we need the eggs."

Teacher: Dennis! When you yawn you should put your hand to your mouth.
Dennis: What, and get it bitten?

"Now remember, boys and girls," said the science teacher. "You can tell a tree's age by counting the rings in a cross-section. One ring for each year." Alec went home for tea and found a Swiss roll on the table. "I'm not eating that, Mom," he said. "It's five years old."

☆ ☆ ☆

A mother was desperate to get her under-age daughter into kindergarten and was trying to impress the principal with the child's intellectual abilities. "She'll easily keep up with the others even though she is a year younger," said the mother.

"Well," said the teacher doubtfully. "Could she prove it by saying something?"

"Certainly, Miss," said the child. "Something pertaining to your conversation or something purely irrelevant?"

☆ ☆ ☆

The class was set an essay on Shakespeare. Jacqui wrote in her book, "Shakespeare wrote tragedy, comedy, and errors."

Did you know that eight out of every ten schoolchildren use ballpoint pens to write with?

Gosh! What do the other two use them for?

☆ ☆ ☆

Knock knock.
Who's there?
Eamon.
Eamon who?
Eamon a good mood – have my
    piece of cake.

Knock knock.
Who's there?
Ear.
Ear who?
Ear you are – a letter.

Knock knock.
Who's there?
Earl.
Earl who?
Earl tell you if you open the door.

Knock knock.
Who's there?
Ears.
Ears who?
Ears looking at you kid.

Knock knock.
Who's there?
Earwig.
Earwig who?
Earwigo!

Geography Teacher: What mineral do we import from America?
Daft Darren: Coca-Cola!

"You never get anything right," complained the teacher. "What kind of job do you think you'll get when you leave school?"
"Well I want to be the weather girl on TV."

☆   ☆   ☆

What did the bookworm say to the school librarian?
Can I burrow this book please?

☆   ☆   ☆

"And what might your name be?" the school secretary asked the new boy. "Well it might be Cornelius, but it's not. It's Sam."

☆   ☆   ☆

Mr Jones, the art teacher, was very small and very meek. One day he found his car smeared with rude words painted bright red. He told the principal, who told the school that unless someone owned up the vacation would be canceled. A few minutes after assembly there was a knock on Mr Jones's door. "Come in!" he called and there was Nigel Hawkins, the school bully – six feet tall and built like a tank.
"It was me that painted the words on your car."
"Oh thank you for confessing," gulped Mr Jones. "I'm not sure that your spelling was 100 per cent accurate, but I thought you'd like to know that I loved the color."

☆   ☆   ☆

Andy: What's the difference between a wage and a salary, Miss?

Teacher: If you earn a wage, you are paid every week, if you earn a salary, you are paid every month. Teachers, for example, get paid salaries because they are paid monthly.

Andy: Please, Miss, where do they work?

"The girl beside me in math is very clever," said Alec to his mother. "She's got enough brain for two."

"Perhaps you'd better think of marriage," said Mom.

☆　☆　☆

"How do you spell 'blancmange'?" the dinner lady asked her assistant when she was chalking up the lunch menu.

"Er . . . b.l.a.m . . . no . . . er b.l.a.a . . . no . . ."

"Never mind," said the dinner lady. "Tony," she shouted to the other assistant, "open a tin of rice pudding will you?"

☆　☆　☆

"Why have you written that Shakespeare was a corset manufacturer before he became a playwright?" asked the English teacher.

"Because he wrote that he could put a girdle round the earth in 40 minutes."

☆　☆　☆

"What shall we play today?" said Theresa to her best friend Emma.

"Let's play schools," said Emma.

"OK!" said Theresa. "But I'm going to be absent."

☆　☆　☆

Knock knock.
Who's there?
Eddie.
Eddie who?
Eddie-body you like.

Knock knock.
Who's there?
Edna.
Edna who?
Edna cloud.

Knock knock.
Who's there?
Edna.
Edna who?
Edna way.

Knock knock.
Who's there?
Edward.
Edward who?
Edward like to play now, please.

Knock knock.
Who's there?
Edwin.
Edwin who?
Edwin a cup if I could run faster.

"Please, Miss! How do you spell 'ichael'?"
The teacher was rather bewildered. "Don't you mean 'Michael'?"
"No, Miss. I've written the 'M' already."

A teacher was correcting exam papers when he came across Alec's effort: a sheet of paper, blank apart from his name and "Macbeth, Act II, Scene V, Line 28." The teacher reached for his Shakespeare and turned to Macbeth where he found that the 28th line of the fifth scene of the second act read, "I cannot do this bloody thing."

"Now don't forget, boys," the science teacher droned on. "If it wasn't for water we would never learn to swim. And if we'd never learned to swim, just think how many people would have drowned!"

At Christmas the school went to a special service in church. The teacher asked if they had enjoyed it, and if they had behaved themselves. "Oh yes, Miss," said Brenda. "A lady came round and offered us a plate full of money, but we all said no thank you."

At graduation day, to mark the end of a particularly trying year, the principal said, "A parent said to me recently that half the teachers do all the work and the other half nothing at all. I'd like to assure all the parents here this afternoon that at this school the opposite is the case."

"I have decided to abolish all corporal punishment at this school," said the principal at morning assembly. "That means that there will be no physical punishment."

"Does that mean that you're stopping school dinners as well, Sir?"

"I want you to help me stop my son gambling," an anxious father said to his boy's principal. "I don't know where he gets it from but it's bet, bet, bet."

"Leave it to me," said the principal. A week later he phoned the boy's father. "I think I've cured him," he said.

"How?"

"Well, I saw him looking at my beard and he said, 'I bet that's a false beard.' 'How much?' I said, and he said '$5.'"

"What happened?" asked the father.

"Well he tugged my beard which is quite natural and I made him give me $5. I'm sure that'll teach him a lesson."

"No it won't," said the father. "He bet me $10 this morning that he'd pull your beard with your permission by the end of the week."

I was doing my homework yesterday and I asked my dad what a circle is. He said it's a round straight line with a hole in the middle.

Pupil to Dinner Lady: Excuse me, but I have a complaint.

Dinner Lady: This is the school dining room, not the doctor's office.

Knock knock.
Who's there?
Eel.
Eel who?
Eel meet again.

Knock knock.
Who's there?
Effie.
Effie who?
Effie'd known you were coming
    he'd have stayed home.

Knock knock.
Who's there?
Egg.
Egg who?
Eggsactly.

Knock knock.
Who's there?
Egbert.
Egbert who?
Egbert no bacon.

Knock knock.
Who's there?
Egypt.
Egypt who?
Egypt me out in the cold!

"Ann!" the teacher shouted one day at the girl who had been daydreaming out the window. "If India has the world's second largest population; oranges are 50 cents for six; and it costs $3 for a day return to Austin – how old am I?"

"32!"

"Why did you say that?"

"Well, my brother's 16 and he's half mad!"

What is the most popular sentence at school?

I don't know.

"I'm not going to school today," Alexander said to his mother. "The teachers bully me and the boys in my class don't like me."

"You're going. And that's final. I'll give you two good reasons why."

"Why?"

"Firstly, you're 35 years old. Secondly, you're the principal."

Some people say the school cook's cooking is out of this world.
Most pupils wish it was out of their stomachs.

Joan's teacher got so fed up of her fooling around in class that he wrote a letter of complaint to her father.

"What's all this about?" roared Dad. "Your teacher says he finds it impossible to teach you anything."

"I told you he was no good," said Joan.

When I was at school I was as smart as the next fellow.
What a pity the next fellow was such an idiot.

Anna: I was top of the class last week.
Mom: How did you manage that?
Anna: I managed to answer a question about elephants.
Mom: What question?
Anna: Well, the teacher asked us how many legs an elephant had, and I said five.
Mom: But that wasn't right.
Anna: I know, but it was the nearest anyone got.

When doing exams Dick knows all the answers.
It's the questions that get him confused.

Teacher: Are you good at arithmetic?
Mary: Well, yes and no.
Teacher: What do you mean, yes and no?
Mary: Yes, I'm no good at arithmetic.

What should you do if you find a gorilla sitting at your school desk?
Sit somewhere else.

Science Teacher: Can you tell me one substance that conducts electricity, Jane?
Jane: Why, er . . .
Science Teacher: Wire is correct.

Knock knock.
Who's there?
Eames.
Eames who?
Eames to please!

Knock knock.
Who's there?
Eight.
Eight who?
Eight me out of house and home.

Knock knock.
Who's there?
Ellie.
Ellie who.
Ellie Phant.

Knock knock.
Who's there?
Miss Ellie.
Miss Ellie who?
Miss Ellie good shows lately?

Knock knock.
Who's there?
Ellis.
Ellis who?
Ellis damnation.

Why is a pencil the heaviest thing in your bag?
Because it's full of lead.

The pupils in the 12th grade, who had learned to type, were being interviewed by prospective employers. Lisa was asked her typing speed. "I'm not sure," she replied. "But I can rub out at 50 words a minute."

Why is a classroom like an old car?
Because it's full of nuts, and has a crank at the front.

Teacher: Who was that on the phone, Samantha?
Samantha: No one important, Miss. Just some man who said it was long distance from Australia, so I told him I knew that already.

Retired colonel, talking of the good old days: Have you ever hunted bear?
His grandson's teacher: No, but I've been fishing in shorts.

Art Teacher: What color would you paint the sun and the wind?
Brian: The sun rose, and the wind blue.

When is a blue school book not a blue school book?
When it is read.

Teacher: You're wearing a very strange pair of socks, Darren. One's blue with red spots, and one's yellow with green stripes.
Darren: Yes, and I've got another pair just the same at home.

Teacher: And did you see the Catskill Mountains on your visit to America?
Jimmy: No, but I saw them kill mice.

Biology Teacher: What kinds of birds do we get in captivity?
Janet: Jail birds, Miss!

What are the small rivers that run into the Nile?
The juve-niles.

Billy: I thought there was a choice for dinner today.
Dinner Lady: There is.
Billy: No, there isn't. There's only cheese pie.
Dinner Lady: You can choose to eat it or leave it.

School Doctor to Parent: I'm afraid your daughter needs glasses.
Parent: How can you tell?
School Doctor: By the way she came in through the window.

Knock knock.
Who's there?
Emil.
Emil who?
Emil would be nice if you've got
    some food.

Knock knock.
Who's there?
Emma.
Emma who?
Emma new neighbor – come round
    for tea.

Knock knock.
Who's there?
Emmett.
Emmett who?
Emmett the front door, not the
    back.

Knock knock.
Who's there?
Enid.
Enid who?
Enid a glass of water.

Knock knock.
Who's there?
Enoch.
Enoch who?
Enoch and Enoch but no one
    answers the door!

Teacher: Eat up your roast beef, it's full of iron.
Dottie: No wonder it's so tough.

What did the children do when there were rock cakes for lunch?
Took their pick.

Why was the cannibal expelled from school?
Because he kept buttering up the teacher.

Teacher: You weren't at school last Friday, Robert. I heard you were out playing football.
Robert: That's not true, Sir. And I've got the baseball tickets to prove it.

Tommy was saying his prayers as his father passed by his bedroom door. "God bless Mommy, and God bless Daddy, and please make Calais the capital of France."
"Tommy," said his father, "why do you want Calais to be the capital of France?"
"Because that's what I wrote in my geography test!"

A school inspector was talking to a pupil. "How many teachers work in this school?" he asked.
"Only about half of them, I reckon," replied the pupil.

Teacher: What is meant by "doggerel"?
Terry: Little dogs, Miss.

What did the dinner lady say when the teacher told her off for putting her finger in his soup?
"It's all right, it isn't hot."

Two girls were talking in the corridor.
"That boy over there is getting on my nerves," said Clarrie.
"But he's not even looking at you," replied Clara.
"That's what's getting on my nerves," retorted Clarrie.

What's black and white and horrible?
A math examination paper.

Teacher: Recite your tables to me, Joan.
Joan: Dining table, kitchen table, bedside table . . .

Teacher: What's the difference between a buffalo and a bison?
Student: You can't wash your hands in a buffalo, Miss.

A motorist approached the principal one afternoon and said, "I'm awfully sorry, but I think I've just run over the school cat. Can I replace it?"
The principal looked him up and down and replied, "I doubt if you'd be the mouser she was."

Knock knock.
Who's there?
Erica.
Erica who?
Erica'd the last sweet.

Knock knock.
Who's there?
Erin.
Erin who?
Erin your lungs.

Knock knock.
Who's there?
Esau.
Esau who?
Esau you in the bath!

Knock knock.
Who's there?
Ethan.
Ethan who?
Ethan people don't go to church.

Knock knock.
Who's there?
Ethan.
Ethan who?
Ethan all my dinner.

Why should a school not be near a chicken farm?
To avoid the pupils overhearing fowl language.

Teacher: Andrew, your homework looks as if it is in your father's handwriting.
Andrew: Well, I used his pen, Sir.

Father: Would you like me to help you with your homework?
Son: No thanks, I'd rather get it wrong by myself.

☆   ☆   ☆

Piano Tuner: I've come to tune the piano.
Music Teacher: But we didn't send for you.
Piano Tuner: No, but the people who live across the street did.

Teacher: What is the longest night of the year?
Alex: A fortnight.

Did you hear about the Inuit teacher who was reciting "Little Jack Horner" to her class of five-year-olds? She'd got as far as "Little Jack Horner sat in a corner" when one little girl put up her hand and said, "Please, Miss, what's a corner?"

How can you save school dumplings from drowning?
Put them in gravy boats.

Why is school like a shower?
One wrong turn and you're in hot water.

How does a Clever Dick spend hours on his homework every night, and yet get twelve hours' sleep?
He puts his homework underneath his mattress.

Darren, at school dinner: I've just swallowed a bone.
Teacher: Are you choking?
Darren: No, I'm serious.

Pupil: Excuse me, Sir, but I don't think I deserve a mark of 0 for this exam paper.
Teacher: Neither do I, but it's the lowest mark I can give.

Was the principal's brother really a missionary?
He certainly was. He gave the people of the Cannibal Islands their first taste of Christianity.

Mary's class was taken to the Natural History Museum in London. "Did you enjoy yourself?" asked her mother when she got home.
"Oh yes," replied Mary. "But it was funny going to a dead zoo."

Knock knock.
Who's there?
Eugene.
Eugene who?
Eugene, me Tarzan.

Knock knock.
Who's there?
Eunice.
Eunice who?
Eunice is like your nephew.

Knock knock.
Who's there?
Eunice.
Eunice who?
Eunice is a witch – I thought you
    should know.

Knock knock.
Who's there?
Euripides.
Euripides who?
Euripides trousers, you pay for a
    new pair.

Knock knock.
Who's there?
Europe.
Europe who?
Europening the door very slowly.

Why is a pupil learning to sing like someone opening a can of sardines? Because they both have trouble with the key.

Sign on the school bulletin board: Guitar for sale, cheap, no strings attached.

Why was Harold called the space cadet when he was at school? Because he had a lot of space between his ears.

When George left school he was going to be a printer.
All the teachers said he was the right type.

Did you hear about the schoolgirl who was so excited about a book she found in the library called "How to Hug"?
It turned out to be volume eight of an encyclopedia.

How can you tell when it's rabbit pie for school dinner?
It has hares in it.

English Teacher: Now give me a sentence using the word "fascinate."
Clara: My raincoat has ten buttons but I can only fasten eight.

Rob: I must rush home and cut the lawn.
Teacher: Did your father promise you something if you cut it?
Rob: No, he promised me something if I didn't!

☆　☆　☆

Jennifer: How come you did so badly in history? I thought you had all the dates written on your sleeve?
Miriam: That's the trouble, I put on my geography blouse by mistake.

PE Master: Why didn't you stop the ball?
Hapless Harold: I thought that was what the net was for.

☆　☆　☆

Nigel: You said the school dentist would be painless, but he wasn't.
Teacher: Did he hurt you?
Nigel: No, but he screamed when I bit his finger.

☆　☆　☆

What's the difference between an iced lolly and the school bully?
You lick one, the other licks you.

☆　☆　☆

Mary arrived home from school covered in spots. "Whatever's the matter?" asked her mother.
"I don't know," replied Mary, "but the teacher thinks I may have caught decimals."

☆　☆　☆

131

Knock knock.
Who's there?
Eva.
Eva who?
Eva had a smack in the mouth?

Knock knock.
Who's there?
Evan.
Evan who?
Evan you should know who it is.

Knock knock.
Who's there?
Evan.
Evan who?
Evan only knows!

Knock knock.
Who's there?
Eve.
Eve who?
Eve-ho, here we go.

Knock knock.
Who's there?
Evie.
Evie who?
Evie weather.

Father: I want to take my girl out of this terrible math class.
Teacher: But she's top of the class.
Father: That's why I think it must be a terrible class.

What can a schoolboy keep and give away at the same time?
A cold.

Teacher: Why do birds fly south in winter?
Jim: Because it's too far to walk.

Knock, knock.
Who's there?
Ida.
Ida who?
Ida nawful time at school today.

Mother: How was your first day at school?
Little Boy: OK, but I haven't got my present yet.
Mother: What do you mean?
Little Boy: Well the teacher gave me a chair, and said "Sit there for the present."

Mother: Did you get a good place in the geography test?
Daughter: Yes, Mom, I sat next to the cleverest kid in the class.

Why did Rupert eat six school dinners?
He wanted to be a big success.

Girl: Mom, you know you're always worried about me failing math?
Mother: Yes.
Girl: Well, your worries are over.

It's a note from the teacher about me telling lies – but it's not true.

Father: This report gives you a D for conduct and an A for courtesy. How on earth did you manage that?
Son: Easy. Whenever I punch someone, I apologize.

Teacher: Who was the first woman on earth?
Angela: I don't know, Sir.
Teacher: Come on, Angela, it has something to do with an apple.
Angela: Granny Smith?

The chemistry teacher added acid from one beaker to a solution in another. Within seconds the classroom was filled with foul-smelling smoke that bubbled out of the beaker. "Now, boys," he spluttered, "I'm going to drop this coin into the beaker. Will it dissolve in the acid?" And as he spoke he plopped the coin into the foaming beaker.
"It definitely won't dissolve, Sir!" said one boy.
"How can you be so sure?" asked the teacher.
"Because if it would, you would never have dropped it in there!"

What key went to university?
A Yale.

Knock knock.
Who's there?
Fang.
Fang who?
Fangs for the memory.

Knock knock.
Who's there?
Farrah.
Farrah who?
Farrah 'nough.

Knock knock.
Who's there?
Fanny.
Fanny who?
Fanny you not knowing who I am!

Knock knock.
Who's there?
Fanta.
Fanta who?
Fanta Claus.

Knock knock.
Who's there?
Fantasy.
Fantasy who?
Fantasy a walk in the park?

Jennifer: Are you coming to my party?
Sandra: No, I ain't going.
Jennifer: Now, you know what Miss told us. Not ain't. It's I am not going, he is not going, she is not going, they are not going.
Sandra: Blimey, ain't nobody going?

Father: Jennifer, I've had a letter from your teacher. It seems you've been neglecting your appearance.
Jennifer: Dad?
Father: He says you haven't appeared in school all week.

Principal: I've called you into my office, Peter, because I want to talk to you about two words I wish you wouldn't use so often. One is "great" and the other is "lousy."
Peter: Certainly Sir. What are they?

☆   ☆   ☆

Wife to Husband: I think Spencer may grow up to be a space scientist. I was talking to his teacher today and she said he was taking up space.

☆   ☆   ☆

Which capital city cheats at exams?
Peking.

☆   ☆   ☆

Teacher: Colin, one of your essays is very good but the other one I can't read.
Colin: Yes, Sir. My mother is a much better writer than my father.

☆   ☆   ☆

Teacher: What happened to your homework?
Boy: I made it into a paper plane and someone hijacked it.

Boy: Why did you throw my homework in the bin?
Teacher: Because it was trash.

☆　☆　☆

Teacher: What's this a picture of?
Class: Don't know, Miss.
Teacher: It's a kangaroo.
Class: What's a kangaroo, Miss?
Teacher: A kangaroo is a native of Australia.
Smallest Boy: Wow, my sister's married one of them!

☆　☆　☆

A little boy came home from his first day at kindergarten and said to his mother, "What's the use of going to school? I can't read, I can't write and the teacher won't let me talk."

☆　☆　☆

Teacher: I'd like to go through one whole day without having to punish you.
Girl: You have my permission, Sir.

☆　☆　☆

Father: I see from your report that you're not doing so well in history. Why's this?
Son: I can't help it. He keeps asking me about things that happened before I was born.

Knock knock.
Who's there?
Felix.
Felix who?
Felixtremely cold.

Knock knock.
Who's there?
Fergie.
Fergie who?
Fergiedness sake let me in!

Knock knock.
Who's there?
Few.
Few who?
Few! What's that smell?

Knock knock.
Who's there?
Fiddle.
Fiddle who?
Fiddle-dee-dee.

Knock knock.
Who's there?
Fido.
Fido who?
Fido known you were coming I'd
    have bolted all the doors.

Mother: What did your father say about your report?
Girl: Well, if you want me to cut out the swear words, he didn't really say anything.

Teacher: What's the best way to pass this geometry test?
Boy: Knowing all the angles?

Girl to Friend: My mom is suffering from a minor neurosis. Every time she sees my report, she faints.

Mother: I told you not to eat cake before supper.
Daughter: But Mom, it's part of my homework. "If you take an eighth of a cake from a whole cake, how much is left?"

☆   ☆   ☆

Mother to Friend: Karen's so imaginative! I asked her what the "F" meant on her report, and she said "fantastic".

Boy to Friend: My dad is so old, when he was at school, history was called current events.

☆   ☆   ☆

Teacher: Were you copying his sums?
Girl: No, Sir. I was just looking to see if he'd got them right.

Teacher: In this exam you will be allowed ten minutes for each question.
Boy: How long is the answer?

Teacher: I told you to write this poem out 20 times because your handwriting is so bad.
Girl: I'm sorry, Miss – my arithmetic's not that good either.

Teacher: Billy. Didn't you hear me call you?
Billy: Yes, Miss, but you told us yesterday not to answer back.

Mother: What do you mean, the school must be haunted?
Daughter: Well, the principal kept going on about the school spirit.

Teacher: I wish you'd pay a little attention.
Girl: I'm paying as little as possible.

Mother: What did you learn at school today?
Son: Not enough. I have to go back tomorrow.

Teacher: Why did you put that frog in Melinda's case?
Boy: Because I couldn't find a mouse.

Knock knock.
Who's there?
Fitzwilliam.
Fitzwilliam who?
Fitzwilliam better than it fits me.

☆   ☆   ☆

Knock knock.
Who's there?
Flea.
Flea who?
Flea blind mice.

☆   ☆   ☆

Knock knock.
Who's there?
Flea.
Flea who?
Flea's a jolly good feller!

☆   ☆   ☆

Knock knock.
Who's there?
Flea.
Flea who?
Flea thirty!

☆   ☆   ☆

Knock knock.
Who's there?
Fletcher.
Fletcher who?
Fletcher stick, there's a good boy.

☆   ☆   ☆

What do you mean, my spelling isn't much good – that's my algebra.

Teacher: You should have been here at nine o'clock.
Boy: Why? Did something happen?

Mother: Do you know a girl named Jenny Simon?
Daughter: Yes, she sleeps next to me in math.

Teacher: If I had ten flies on my desk, and I killed one, how many flies would be left?
Girl: One – the dead one!

One unfortunate teacher started off a lesson with the following instruction: "I want you all to give me a list of the lower animals, starting with Georgina Clark . . ."

Teacher: You seem to be exceedingly ignorant, Williams. Have you read Dickens?
Williams: No, Sir.
Teacher: Have you read Shakespeare?
Williams: No, Sir.
Teacher: Well, what have you read?
Williams: Er . . . er . . . I've red hair, Sir.

☆ ☆ ☆

"How do you spell wrong?"
"R-o-n-g."
"That's wrong."
"That's what you asked for, isn't it?"

☆ ☆ ☆

Music Master: Brian, if "f" means "forte," what does "ff" mean?
Brian: Eighty!

"Sir!" said Alexander. "Empty Coke tins, fish-and-chip papers, plastic bags, used tissues, broken bottles, empty boxes . . ."
"Alexander!" snapped the teacher. "You're talking garbage again!"

"Anne, can you spell 'banana' for me?"
"Well, Sir, I know how to start, but I don't know when to stop!"

"Philip," asked the chemistry teacher, "what is HNO_3?"
"Oh, er . . . just a minute, Miss, er . . . it's on the tip of my tongue . . ."
"Well in that case – spit it out. It's nitric acid!"

☆   ☆   ☆

Miss: Why do we put a hyphen in a bird-cage?
Stella: For a parrot to perch on, Miss.

Knock knock.
Who's there?
Flute.
Flute who?
Flute in the basement –
   everything's wet.

Knock knock.
Who's there?
Fly.
Fly who?
Fly away soon.

Knock knock.
Who's there?
Fonda.
Fonda who?
Fonda my family.

Knock knock.
Who's there?
Foot.
Foot who?
Foot two pence I'd go away now.

Knock knock.
Who's there?
Fork.
Fork who?
Forket her – she wasn't worth it.

144

Teacher: Mason, what is the outer part of a tree called?
Mason: Don't know, Sir.
Teacher: Bark, boy, bark!
Mason: Woof-woof!

"Frank," said the weary math teacher, "if you had seven dollars in your pocket, and seven dollars in another pocket, what would you have?"
"Someone else's trousers on!"

Good news! At school today there will be free Coca-Cola for everyone . . . the bad news is that straws are 50 cents each!

The five-year-olds had been told to draw a scene representing the flight into Egypt. One little tot proudly displayed a drawing of a jumbo jet containing the three members of the Holy Family – but also a fourth figure. "When I said 'flight,' I didn't quite mean a jet plane," said the teacher. "However, we'll let that pass for now. But who is the fourth person on the plane?"
To which the little one replied, "That's Pontius Pilate."

Teacher: What came after the Stone Age and the Bronze Age?
Pupil: The sausage.

What did you learn in school today, son?

I learned that those sums you did for me were wrong!

School meals are not generally popular with those that have to eat them, and sometimes with good reason. "What kind of pie do you call this?" asked one schoolboy indignantly.

"What's it taste of?" asked the cook.

"Glue!"

"Then it's apple pie – the plum pie tastes of soap."

Teacher: What family does the octopus belong to?

Pupil: Nobody I know.

Teacher: Does anyone know which month has 28 days?

Pupil: All of them!

"Any complaints?" asked the teacher during school dinner.

"Yes, Sir," said one bold lad, "these peas are awfully hard, Sir."

The master dipped a spoon into the peas on the boy's plate and tasted them. "They seem soft enough to me," he declared.

"Yes, they are now, I've been chewing them for the last half-hour."

Knock knock.
Who's there?
Fred.
Fred who?
Fred I've got some bad news.

Knock knock.
Who's there?
Frank.
Frank who?
Frank you very much.

Knock knock.
Who's there?
Fred.
Fred who?
Fred this needle – I'm cross-eyed.

Knock knock.
Who's there?
Franz.
Franz who?
Franz, Romans, countrymen, lend
   me your ears.

Knock knock.
Who's there?
Freddie.
Freddie who?
Freddie won't come out to play
   today.

Knock knock.
Who's there?
Freddie.
Freddie who?
Freddie, steady, go!

Knock knock.
Who's there?
Freddie and Abel.
Freddie and Abel who?
Freddie and Abel to do business.

Knock knock.
Who's there?
Friends.
Friends who?
Friends-ied attack.

Knock knock.
Who's there?
Fruit.
Fruit who?
Fruit of all evil.

Knock knock.
Who's there?
Fudge.
Fudge who?
Fudge up – there's no room!

Teacher: What is the plural of mouse?
Infant: Mice.
Teacher: And what is the plural of baby?
Infant: Twins.

"Alfred, if I had 20 marbles in my right trousers pocket, 20 marbles in my left trousers pocket, 40 marbles in my right hip pocket and 40 marbles in my left hip pocket – what would I have?"
"Heavy trousers, Sir!"

Teacher: Anyone here quick at picking up music?
Terence and Tony: I am, Sir!
Teacher: Right, you two. Move that piano!

Teacher: Alan, give me a sentence starting with "I".
Alan: I is . . .
Teacher: No, Alan. You must always say "I am."
Alan: Oh right. I am the ninth letter of the alphabet.

Teacher: What is a Red Indian's wife called?
Girl: A squaw, Miss.
Teacher: Quite right. And what are Red Indian babies called?
Girl: Squawkers?

Knock knock.
Who's there?
Gail.
Gail who?
Gail of laughter.

Knock knock.
Who's there?
Galway.
Galway who?
Galway you silly boy.

Knock knock.
Who's there?
Gandhi.
Gandhi who?
Gandhi come out to play?

Knock knock.
Who's there?
Gary.
Gary who?
Gary on smiling.

Knock knock.
Who's there?
Gaskill.
Gaskill who?
Gaskills if it's not turned off.

Knock knock.
Who's there?
Gazza.
Gazza who?
Gazza kiss.

Knock knock.
Who's there?
Genoa.
Genoa who?
Genoa good teacher?

Knock knock.
Who's there?
Geoff.
Geoff who?
Geoff feel like going out tonight?

Knock knock.
Who's there?
Gerald.
Gerald who?
Gerald man from round the corner.

Knock knock.
Who's there?
Germaine.
Germaine who?
Germaine you don't recognize me?

Teacher: Martin, I've taught you everything I know, and you're still ignorant!

Teacher: Tommy Russell, you're late again.
Tommy: Sorry, Sir. It's my bus – it's always coming late.
Teacher: Well, if it's late again tomorrow, catch an earlier one.

Teacher: Ford, you're late for school again. What is it this time?
Ford: I sprained my ankle, Sir.
Teacher: That's a lame excuse.

Teacher: Now, Harrison, if your father borrows $10 from me and pays me back at $1 a month, at the end of six months how much will he owe me?
Harrison: $10, Sir.
Teacher: I'm afraid you don't know much about arithmetic, Harrison.
Harrison: I'm afraid you don't know much about my father!

Teacher: Carol, what is "can't" short for?
Carol: Cannot.
Teacher: And what is "don't" short for?
Carol: Doughnut!

Knock knock.
Who's there?
Gertie.
Gertie who?
Gertiesy call.

Knock knock.
Who's there?
Ghana.
Ghana who?
Ghana get me some wheels and hit
    the town!

Knock knock.
Who's there?
Ghent.
Ghent who?
Ghent out of town.

Knock knock.
Who's there?
Ghost.
Ghost who?
Ghost town.

Knock knock.
Who's there?
Ghoul.
Ghoul who?
Ghoulpost painter.

"Do you know," said the teacher to one of her pupils, "that we call you 'the wonder child' in the staff room?"
"Why's that, Miss?"
"Because we all wonder when you're going to wash!"

Teacher: Spell the word "needle," Kenneth.
Kenneth: N-e-i-
Teacher: No, Kenneth, there's no "i" in needle.
Kenneth: Then it's a rotten needle, Miss!

Cookery Mistress: Helen, what are the best things to put in a fruit cake?
Helen: Teeth!

Andy was late for school. "Andy!" roared his mother. "Have you got your socks on yet?"
"Yes, Mom," replied Andy. "All except one."

"Simon's a bully and thinks he's really hard."
"He will be when we've poured this concrete over him."

Teacher: Matthew, what is the climate of New Zealand?
Matthew: Very cold, sir.
Teacher: Wrong.
Matthew: But, Sir! When they send us meat, it always arrives frozen!

Teacher: What's the difference between the death rate in Elizabethan times and the death rate nowadays?
Smart Sue: It's the same, Miss – one death per person.

Celia: The food at our school is terrible.
Amelia: Yes, even the trash cans get indigestion.

☆   ☆   ☆

What's the difference between a bully and a bogey?
A bogey only gets up your nose sometimes.

☆   ☆   ☆

Dave: What did your teacher say when you took your pet bulldog to school?
Don: He said, "You can't bring that ugly brute in here."
Dave: What happened then?
Don: The bulldog said, "It's not my fault, he brought me."

Clara: I'm so bright I'm going to cut down my studying time by half.
Sarah: Which half are you going to cut out – thinking about studying or talking about studying?

Knock knock.
Who's there?
Giuseppe.
Giuseppe who?
Giuseppe credit cards?

Knock knock.
Who's there?
Gladys.
Gladys who?
Gladys letter isn't a bill.

Knock knock.
Who's there?
Glasgow.
Glasgow who?
Glasgow to the theater.

Knock knock.
Who's there?
Goose.
Goose who?
Goose who's knocking at the door!

Knock knock.
Who's there?
Gopher.
Gopher who?
Gopher help – I'm stuck in the mud.

What is a termite's favorite breakfast?
Oak-meal.

What did one termite say to the other termite when he saw a house burning?
Barbecue tonight!

What's the difference between a fly and an elephant?
Quite a lot really.

What do you call an amorous insect?
The Love Bug.

What do you call an insect that has just flown by?
A flu bug.

What did the termite say in the pub?
"Is the bar tender here?"

What did the termite say when he saw that his friends had completely eaten a chair?
"Wooden you know it!"

What was the snail doing on the freeway?
About one mile a day.

How do you keep flies out of the kitchen?
Put a bucket of manure in the lounge.

☆　☆　☆

What is the definition of a slug?
A snail with a housing problem.

☆　☆　☆

How do snails get their shells all shiny?
They use snail polish.

☆　☆　☆

Where do you find giant snails?
On the end of a giant's fingers.

☆　☆　☆

What gas do snails prefer?
Shell.

☆　☆　☆

What do you get if you cross a bottle of water with an electric eel?
A bit of a shock really!

☆　☆　☆

What do you get if you cross an eel with a shopper?
A slippery customer.

☆　☆　☆

How did the clever snail carry his home?
He used a snail trailer.

☆　☆　☆

Knock knock.
Who's there?
Greene.
Greene who?
Greene is my valley.

Knock knock.
Who's there?
Gray.
Gray who?
Grayt balls of fire!

Knock knock.
Who's there?
Greg.
Greg who?
Greg Scott!

Knock knock.
Who's there?
Greece.
Greece who?
Greece my palm and I'll tell you.

Knock knock.
Who's there?
Greta.
Greta who?
Greta job.

What did the cowboy maggot say when he went into the saloon bar?
"Gimme a slug of whiskey."

☆　☆　☆

What kind of fish goes well with ice cream?
A jelly fish.

What do you call a mosquito on vacation?
An itch-hiker.

☆　☆　☆

What is the glowworms' favorite song?
'Wake Me Up Before You Glow Glow' by Wham!

☆　☆　☆

What do you get if you cross the Lone Ranger with an insect?
The Masked-quito.

☆　☆　☆

What has antlers and sucks your blood?
A moose-quito.

☆　☆　☆

Why didn't the two worms go into Noah's ark in an apple?
Because everyone had to go in pairs.

☆　☆　☆

What do worms leave round their bathtubs?
The scum of the earth.

☆　☆　☆

How do you make a glowworm happy?
Cut off its tail. It'll be de-lighted.

☆　☆　☆

How can you tell which end of a worm is its head?
Tickle its middle and see which end smiles.

What do you get if you cross a worm with a young goat?
A dirty kid.

What did one maggot say to the other who was stuck in an apple?
"Worm your way out of that one, then!"

One worm said to the other, "I love you, I love you, I love you."
"Don't be stupid," the other worm said, "I'm your other end!"

What do you get if you cross a glowworm with a pint of beer?
Light ale.

Why was the glowworm unhappy?
Because her children were not very bright.

What did the woodworm say to the chair?
"It's been nice gnawing you!"

What did the dog say to the flea?
Stop bugging me.

Knock knock.
Who's there?
Grimm.
Grimm who?
Grimm and bear it.

Knock knock.
Who's there?
Grub.
Grub who?
Grub hold of my hand and let's go!

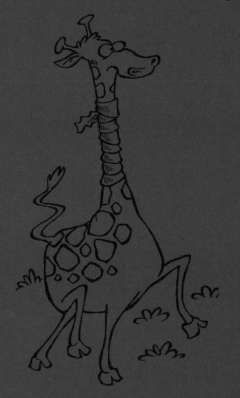

Knock knock.
Who's there?
Guinea.
Guinea who?
Guinea a high five!

Knock knock.
Who's there?
Guinevere.
Guinevere who?
Guinevere going to get together?

Knock knock.
Who's there?
Gus.
Gus who?
Gus what – it's me!

When should you stop for a glowworm?
When he has a red light.

☆   ☆   ☆

What's worse than finding a maggot in your apple?
Finding half a maggot in your apple.

☆   ☆   ☆

What did one maggot say to another?
"What's a nice girl like you doing in a joint like this?"

☆   ☆   ☆

What's yellow, wiggly and dangerous?
A maggot with a bad attitude.

☆   ☆   ☆

What do you get if you cross a glowworm with a python?
A twenty-foot long strip light that can squeeze you to death.

☆   ☆   ☆

Why wouldn't they let the butterfly into the dance?
Because it was a moth ball.

Why are glowworms good to carry in your bag?
They can lighten your load.

☆   ☆   ☆

What is a worm's favorite pasta?
Wriggle-toni.

☆   ☆   ☆

What did the bus driver say to the frog?
"Hop on."

What creepie crawlies do athletes break?
Tapeworms.

☆　　☆　　☆

Who is the worms' Prime Minister?
Maggot Thatcher.

☆　　☆　　☆

What's the maggot army called?
The apple corps.

☆　　☆　　☆

What did one worm say to another when he was late home?
"Why in earth are you late?"

☆　　☆　　☆

What's the difference between a worm and a gooseberry?
Ever tried eating worm pie?

☆　　☆　　☆

What do you get if you cross a worm with an elephant?
Big holes in your garden.

☆　　☆　　☆

What is the best advice to give a worm?
Sleep late.

☆　　☆　　☆

What do clever bookworms win?
The Booker Prize.

☆　　☆　　☆

Knock knock.
Who's there?
Haden.
Haden who?
Haden in the bushes.

Knock knock.
Who's there?
Hair.
Hair who?
Hair you go!

Knock knock.
Who's there?
Haiti.
Haiti who?
Haitit when you talk like that!

Knock knock.
Who's there?
Haiti.
Haiti who?
Haiti-nything to do with witches!

Knock knock.
Who's there?
Hallie.
Hallie who?
Hallie-tosis – your breath smells
    awful!

Why do worms taste like chewing gum?
Because they're Wrigley's.

Why did the sparrow fly into the library?
It was looking for bookworms.

What lives in apples and is an avid reader?
A bookworm.

Why do elephants have trunks?
Because they don't have glove compartments.

What makes a glowworm glow?
A light meal.

What do you say if you meet a toad?
"Wart's new?"

One woodworm met another. "How's life?" she asked.
"Oh, same as usual," he replied, "boring."

What would you do if you found a bookworm chewing your favorite book?
Take the words right out of its mouth.

What is a bookworm's idea of a big feast?
War and Peace.

What did one glowworm say to another when his light went out?
"Give me a push, my battery is dead."

☆   ☆   ☆

What do you get if you cross an electric eel and a sponge?
Shock absorbers.

☆   ☆   ☆

What do you call a girl with a frog on her head?
Lily.

What did the jellyfish say when she saw the electric eel?
"How shocking!"

☆   ☆   ☆

How do eels get around the seabed?
They go by octobus.

☆   ☆   ☆

Who was wet and slippery and invaded England?
William the Conger.

☆   ☆   ☆

What is wet and slippery and likes Latin American music?
A conga eel.

☆   ☆   ☆

What's wet and wiggly and says "How do you do?" 16 times?
Two octopuses shaking hands.

☆   ☆   ☆

Knock knock.
Who's there?
Harmony.
Harmony who?
Harmony times must I tell you not to
 do that!

☆　☆　☆

Knock knock.
Who's there?
Harp.
Harp who?
Harp the Herald Angels Sing!

☆　☆　☆

Knock knock.
Who's there?
Hardy.
Hardy who?
Hardy annual.

☆　☆　☆

Knock knock.
Who's there?
Harriet.
Harriet who?
Harriet up!

Knock knock.
Who's there?
Harlow.
Harlow who?
Harlow can you get?

☆　☆　☆

☆　☆　☆

Why do mice need oiling?
Because they squeak.

What is an eel's favorite song?
'Slip Sliding Away.'

☆ ☆ ☆

What do insects learn at school?
Mothematics.

☆ ☆ ☆

What insect lives on nothing?
A moth, because it eats holes.

☆ ☆ ☆

How can you make a moth ball?
Hit it with a fly-swatter.

☆ ☆ ☆

What is pretty and delicate and
carries a sub-machine gun?
A killer butterfly.

☆ ☆ ☆

How do you make a butterfly?
Flick it out of the dish with a butter
knife.

☆ ☆ ☆

What do you get if you cross a moth
with a firefly?
An insect that can find its way
around a dark wardrobe.

☆ ☆ ☆

How do stones stop moths eating your
clothes?
Because a rolling stone gathers no
moths.

☆ ☆ ☆

What likes to spend the summer in a fur coat and the winter in a swimsuit?
A moth.

Why did the moth nibble a hole in the carpet?
He wanted to see the floor show.

What do you get if you cross a snake with a Lego set?
A boa constructor.

☆ ☆ ☆

Why do babies like cobras?
Because they come with their own rattle.

Why wouldn't the snake go on the "speak-your-weight" machine?
He had his own scales.

What do snakes write on the bottom of their letters?
"With love and hisses."

☆ ☆ ☆

What kind of musical instrument do rats play?
The mouse organ.

☆ ☆ ☆

"Dad, is an ox a sort of male cow?"
"Sort of, yes."
"And 'equine' means something to do with horses, doesn't it?"
"That's right."
"So what's an equinox?"

Knock knock.
Who's there?
Hazel.
Hazel who?
Hazel restrict your vision.

☆　☆　☆

Knock knock.
Who's there?
Heather.
Heather who?
Heather pothtman come yet?

☆　☆　☆

Knock knock.
Who's there?
Hedda.
Hedda who?
Hedda ball in goal.

☆　☆　☆

Knock knock.
Who's there?
Heidi.
Heidi who?
Heidi hi campers!

☆　☆　☆

Knock knock.
Who's there?
Heidi.
Heidi who?
Heidi Clare war on you.

What is a myth?
A female moth.

Who do all moths bow to?
The Moth-er Superior.

Why was the moth so unpopular?
He kept picking holes in everything.

What is the biggest moth?
A mam-moth.

How can you tell if a snake is a baby snake?
It has a rattle.

Why did the cat join the Red Cross?
Because she wanted to be a first-aid kit.

What's another word for a python?
A mega-bite.

How do you know that owls are cleverer than chickens?
Have you ever heard of Kentucky Fried Owl?

What did the snake say when he was offered a piece of cheese for dinner?
"Thank you, I'll just have a slither."

What do you get if you cross a serpent and a trumpet?
A snake in the brass.

Which hand would you use to grab a poisonous snake?
Your enemy's.

What is a bat's favorite sport?
Batminton.

What do you do if you find a black mamba in your bathroom?
Wait until he's finished.

What goes dot-dot-croak?
Morse toad.

☆   ☆   ☆

What is a snake's favorite opera?
"Wriggletto."

☆   ☆   ☆

Why did the two boa constrictors get married?
Because they had a crush on each other.

☆   ☆   ☆

What should you do if you find a snake in your bed?
Sleep in the wardrobe.

Knock knock.
Who's there?
Hiram.
Hiram who?
Hiram and fire 'em.

Knock knock.
Who's there?
Hobbit.
Hobbit who?
Hobbit-forming.

Knock knock.
Who's there?
Holly.
Holly who?
Hollylujah!

Knock knock.
Who's there?
Honda.
Honda who?
Honda stand what I'm talking
    about?

Knock knock.
Who's there?
Hope.
Hope who?
Hope you'll have me.

How can you prevent an elephant from charging?
Take away his credit card.

What do you call a snake that is trying to become a bird?
A feather boa.

☆　☆　☆

What is a snake's favorite dance?
Snake, rattle and roll.

☆　☆　☆

Why can't you trust snakes?
They speak with forked tongue.

☆　☆　☆

Have you heard the joke about the slippery eel?
You wouldn't grasp it.

☆　☆　☆

What snakes are good at sums?
Adders.

☆　☆　☆

What do you get if you cross a snake with a hotdog?
A fangfurter.

☆　☆　☆

What do you get if you cross a bag of snakes with a cupboard of food?
Snakes and Larders.

☆　☆　☆

What do you get if you cross a snake with a pig?
A boar constrictor.

☆　☆　☆

Knock knock.
Who's there?
Howard.
Howard who?
Howard you like to stand out here in
    the cold while some idiot keeps
    saying "Who's there?"

Knock knock.
Who's there?
Howie.
Howie who?
Fine thanks. How are you?

Knock knock.
Who's there?
Howl.
Howl who?
Howl I know when it's supper time?

Knock knock.
Who's there?
Huey.
Huey who?
Who am I? I'm me!

Knock knock.
Who's there?
Hugh.
Hugh who?
Hugh wouldn't believe it if I told you.

Knock knock.
Who's there?
Ian.
Ian who?
Ian a lot of money.

Knock knock.
Who's there?
Ice cream.
Ice cream who?
Ice cream loudly.

Knock knock.
Who's there?
Ida.
Ida who?
Ida thought you could say please.

Knock knock.
Who's there?
I4.
I4 who?
I4 the ladies.

☆   ☆   ☆

Knock knock.
Who's there?
Ida.
Ida who?
Ida bought a different knocker if I'd
    been you.

☆   ☆   ☆

What birds spend all their time on their knees?
Birds of prey.

☆   ☆   ☆

Why are snakes hard to fool?
They have no leg to pull.

☆   ☆   ☆

What did the python say when it sneezed?
Ex-squeeze me.

☆   ☆   ☆

What perfume do lady snakes like to wear?
'Poison' by Dior.

☆   ☆   ☆

What is the snake's favorite TV program?
Monty Python.

☆   ☆   ☆

What do you get if you cross an owl with a witch?
A bird that's ugly but doesn't give a hoot.

What do you call a python with a great bedside manner?
A snake charmer.

☆   ☆   ☆

Why did the viper want to become a python?
He got the coiling.

☆   ☆   ☆

What do most people do when they see a python?
They re-coil.

☆   ☆   ☆

What did the snake say to the cornered rat?
"Hiss is the end of the line, mate!"

☆　☆　☆

What do married snakes have on their bath towels?
"Hiss and Hers."

☆　☆　☆

What do you call a snake that informs the police?
A grass-snake.

☆　☆　☆

What do you call a very rude bird?
A mockingbird.

☆　☆　☆

What kind of snake is useful on your windshield?
A viper.

☆　☆　☆

What did the mommy snake say to the crying baby snake?
"Stop crying and viper your nose."

☆　☆　☆

What's the best thing about deadly snakes?
They've got poisonality.

☆　☆　☆

When it is unlucky to see a black cat?
When you're a mouse.

Knock knock.
Who's there?
Ina Minnie.
Ina Minnie who?
Ina Minnie miney mo.

Knock knock.
Who's there?
India.
India who?
India there's a bag belonging to me.

Knock knock.
Who's there?
Ines.
Ines who?
Inespecial place I'll hide your
    present.

Knock knock.
Who's there?
Ingrid.
Ingrid who?
Ingrid sorrow I have to leave you.

Knock knock.
Who's there?
Insect.
Insect who?
Insect your name and address here.

What's the snake's favorite dance?
The mamba.

☆　☆　☆

What's the snake's second favorite
dance?
The shuffle.

☆　☆　☆

How do you get milk from a cat?
Steal her saucer.

Why did the python do National
Service?
He was coiled up.

☆　☆　☆

What's a python's favorite flower?
Coily-flowers.

☆　☆　☆

What do you get if you cross two
snakes with a magic spell?
Addercadabra and abradacobra.

☆　☆　☆

What is a snake's favorite game?
Snakes and Ladders.

☆　☆　☆

What would you get if you crossed a
new-born snake with a basketball?
A bouncing baby boa.

☆　☆　☆

What happened when a deadly
rattlesnake bit a witch?
He died in agony.

☆　☆　☆

Why did the witch feed her cat with cents?
She wanted to put them in the kitty.

Why didn't the viper viper nose?
Because the adder adder handkerchief.

☆　☆　☆

What song do snakes like to sing?
'Viva Aspaña.'

☆　☆　☆

What do you give a sick snake?
Asp-rin.

☆　☆　☆

What did one snake say when the other snake asked him the time?
"Don't asp me!"

☆　☆　☆

What kind of letters did the snake get from his admirers?
Fang mail.

☆　☆　☆

What is a snake's favorite plant?
An asp-idistra.

☆　☆　☆

What's long and green and goes hith?
A snake with a lisp.

☆　☆　☆

Knock knock.
Who's there?
Isabel.
Isabel who?
Isabel necessary on a bicycle?

Knock knock.
Who's there?
Isabella.
Isabella who?
Isabella dingdong?

Knock knock.
Who's there?
Iris.
Iris who?
Iris you would open the door.

Knock knock.
Who's there?
Isadore.
Isadore who?
Isadore on the right way round?

Knock knock.
Who's there?
Isaac.
Isaac who?
Isaac all my staff today.

☆ ☆ ☆

What do baby pythons play with?
Rattle-snakes.

"So glad to meet you," said the fakir politely.
"Charmed I'm sure," replied the snake.

What do you call a rich frog?
A gold-blooded reptile.

What powerful reptile is found in the Sydney Opera House?
The Lizard of Oz.

What's the definition of a nervous breakdown?
A chameleon on a tartan rug.

Why did some snakes disobey Noah when he told them to "go forth and multiply"?
They couldn't – they were adders.

What kind of tiles can't you stick on the wall?
Rep-tiles.

What do you call a cat with eight legs that likes to swim?
An Octopuss.

How do frogs manage to lay so many eggs?
They sit eggsaminations.

☆　　☆　　☆

When is a car like a frog?
When it's being toad.

☆　　☆　　☆

What kind of bull doesn't have horns?
A bullfrog.

☆　　☆　　☆

What do principals and bullfrogs have in common?
Both have a big head that consists mostly of mouth.

☆　　☆　　☆

What jumps up and down in front of a car?
Froglights.

☆　　☆　　☆

What do you call a cat that drinks vinegar?
A sour puss.

Where does a ten-tonne frog sleep?
Anywhere it wants to!

☆　　☆　　☆

What happened to the lizard in the wizard's garden pond?
He had him newt-ered.

☆　　☆　　☆

What do you say to a hitch-hiking frog?
"Hop in!"

☆　　☆　　☆

Knock knock.
Who's there?
Jack.
Jack who?
Jack in the box.

Knock knock.
Who's there?
Jackie.
Jackie who?
Jackie'n that job – it's killing you.

Knock knock.
Who's there?
Jacqueline.
Jacqueline who?
Jacqueline Hyde.

Knock knock.
Who's there?
Jade.
Jade who?
Jade a whole pie today.

Knock knock.
Who's there?
Jagger.
Jagger who?
Jaggered edge.

What has four legs, a tail, whiskers and flies?
A dead cat.

Why do frogs have webbed feet?
To stamp out forest fires.

Why did the toad become a lighthouse keeper?
He had his own frog-horn.

What happened when the frog joined the cricket team?
He bowled long hops.

☆　☆　☆

What did one frog say to the other?
"Time's sure fun when you're having flies!"

☆　☆　☆

What do you get if you cross a frog with a ferry?
A hoppercraft.

☆　☆　☆

What do you call a frog who wants to be a cowboy?
Hoppalong Cassidy.

☆　☆　☆

What is a frog's favorite dance?
The Lindy Hop.

☆　☆　☆

What happens to illegally parked frogs?
They get toad away.

Why did the lizard go on a diet?
It weighed too much for its scales.

What's green and can jump a mile a minute?
A frog with hiccups.

Why was the frog down-in-the-mouth?
He was un-hoppy.

What game do elephants play when they are in a car?
Squash.

What did the croaking frog say to his friend?
"I think I've got a person in my throat."

What's green and goes round and round at 60 miles an hour?
A frog in a blender.

What is yellow and goes round and round at 60 miles an hour?
A moldy frog in a blender.

Why is a frog luckier than a cat?
Because a frog croaks all the time – a cat only croaks nine times.

What would you get if you crossed a frog with a little dog?
A croaker spaniel.

Knock knock.
Who's there?
Jam.
Jam who?
Jam mind! I'm trying to think out
here.

Knock knock.
Who's there?
Jamaica.
Jamaica who?
Jamaica mistake again?

Knock knock.
Who's there?
Jamie.
Jamie who?
Jamie'n you don't recognize my
voice?

Knock knock.
Who's there?
James.
James who?
James people play.

Knock knock.
Who's there?
Jan.
Jan who?
Jan and bread.

How do frogs die?
They Kermit suicide.

Why doesn't Kermit like elephants?
They always want to play leapfrog with
him.

What's the difference between fleas
and dogs?
Dogs can have fleas but fleas can't
have dogs.

What do frogs drink?
Hot croako.

What is a frog's favorite game?
Croak-et.

What is a frog's favorite flower?
The croakus.

What do you get if you cross a planet
with a toad?
Star warts.

What do Scottish toads play?
Hop-scotch.

Jim: Our dog is just like one of the family.
Fred: Which one?

What is a toad's favorite ballet?
Swamp Lake.

What do you call the English Toad Prize-giving ceremony?
The Brit A-warts.

How do toads travel?
By hoppercraft.

What do toads drink?
Croaka-cola.

Where do frogs keep their treasure?
In the croak of gold at the end of the rainbow.

☆   ☆   ☆

What is green and slimy and is found at the North Pole?
A lost frog.

☆   ☆   ☆

What kind of shoes do frogs like?
Open-toad sandals.

☆   ☆   ☆

What do you call a frog spy?
A croak and dagger agent.

Knock knock.
Who's there?
Jay.
Jay who?
Jay what you mean.

Knock knock.
Who's there?
Jay.
Jay who?
Jaylbird with clanking chains.

Knock knock.
Who's there?
Jean.
Jean who?
Jeanius – you just don't
    recognize it.

Knock knock.
Who's there?
Jeanette.
Jeanette who?
Jeanette has too many holes in it,
    the fish will escape.

Knock knock.
Who's there?
Jeff.
Jeff who?
Jeff fancy going out tonight?

What do you call an eighty-year-old frog?
An old croak.

☆   ☆   ☆

What is a toad's favorite sweet?
Lollihops.

☆   ☆   ☆

What do you get if you cross a toad with a mist?
Kermit the Fog.

☆   ☆   ☆

What is a mouse's favorite record?
'Please cheese me.'

☆   ☆   ☆

What's a rat's least favorite record?
'What's new, Pussycat?'

☆   ☆   ☆

What was the name of the movie about a killer lion that swam under water?
Claws.

How do you save a drowning rodent?
Use mouse to mouse resuscitation.

☆   ☆   ☆

How do hens dance?
Chick to chick.

☆   ☆   ☆

What do bees do if they want to use public transport?
Wait at a buzz stop.

☆   ☆   ☆

What do you get if you cross a bee
with a skunk?
A creature that stinks and stings.

What does a queen bee do when she
belches?
She issues a royal pardon.

Who is the bees' favorite composer?
Bee-thoven.

What's yellow and brown and covered
in blackberries?
A bramble bee.

What is more dangerous than being
with a fool?
Fooling with a bee.

☆　　☆　　☆

Why did the bee start spouting
poetry?
He was waxing lyrical.

How does a queen bee get around
the hive?
She's throne.

☆　　☆　　☆

Can bees fly in the rain?
Not without their little yellow jackets.

☆　　☆　　☆

What do you get if you pour hot water
down a rabbit hole?
Hot cross bunnies!

Knock knock.
Who's there?
Jerry.
Jerry who?
Jerry cake.

Knock knock.
Who's there?
Jess.
Jess who?
Jess li'l ol' me.

Knock knock.
Who's there?
Jess.
Jess who?
Don't know, you tell me.

Knock knock.
Who's there?
Jesse.
Jesse who?
Jesse if you can recognize my voice.

Knock knock.
Who's there?
Jessica.
Jessica who?
Jessica lot up last night?

What do you get if you cross a skunk and an owl?
A bird that smells but doesn't give a hoot!

What did the mommy bee say to the naughty little bee?
"Bee-hive yourself!"

☆   ☆   ☆

What goes "hum-choo, hum-choo"?
A bee with a cold.

☆   ☆   ☆

What is a beeline?
The shortest distance between two buzz stops.

☆   ☆   ☆

What's the difference between a very old, shaggy Yeti and a dead bee?
One's a seedy beast and the other's a deceased bee.

☆   ☆   ☆

Who wrote books for little bees?
Bee-trix Potter.

☆   ☆   ☆

What do you call a bee who's had a spell put on him?
Bee-witched.

☆   ☆   ☆

What has brown and yellow stripes and buzzes along at the bottom of the sea?
A bee in a submarine.

☆   ☆   ☆

Why do bees hum?
Because they've forgotten the words.

☆   ☆   ☆

What kind of bee hums and drops things?
A fumble bee.

What did the bee say to the flower?
"Hello, honey."

What are bees' favorite flowers?
Bee-gonias.

What do you get if you cross a kangaroo and a sheep?
A woolly jumper.

Why are black cats such good singers?
They're very mewsical.

What do you call it when a witch's cat falls off her broomstick?
A catastrophe.

What do you get if you cross a witch's cat with Father Christmas?
Santa Claws.

☆   ☆   ☆

What do cats eat for breakfast?
Mice Krispies.

☆   ☆   ☆

What do you get if you cross a witch's cat with a canary?
A peeping tom.

Knock knock.
Who's there?
Jimmy.
Jimmy who?
Jimmy all your money.

Knock knock.
Who's there?
Joan.
Joan who?
Joan you know your own daughter?

Knock knock.
Who's there?
Joan.
Joan who?
Joan call us, we'll call you.

Knock knock.
Who's there?
Joan.
Joan who?
Joan rush, I'll tell you in a minute.

Knock knock.
Who's there?
Joanna.
Joanna who?
Joanna big kiss?

Why do cats never shave?
Because eight out of ten cats prefer
Whiskas.

What did the cat say to the fish
head?
"I've got a bone to pick with you."

☆   ☆   ☆

Why is a kitten like an unhealed
wound?
Both are a little pussy.

☆   ☆   ☆

What do you call a cat that never
comes when it's called?
Im-puss-ible.

☆   ☆   ☆

How does a Yeti get to work?
By icicle.

☆   ☆   ☆

Now you see it. . .now you don't –
what are you looking at?
A black cat walking over a zebra
crossing.

What has four legs, a tail, whiskers
and goes round and round for hours?
A cat in a tumble-drier.

Two caterpillars were crawling along a
twig when a butterfly flew by. "You
know," said one caterpillar to the
other, "when I grow up, you'll never get
me in one of those things."

199

What has four legs, a tail, whiskers and cuts grass?
A lawn miaower.

What do you get if you cross a cat and a canary?
A cat with a full tummy.

What do you call a witch's cat with no legs?
Anything you like – she won't be able to come anyway.

What happened when the cat ate a ball of wool?
She had mittens.

What's furry, has whiskers and chases outlaws?
A posse cat.

What dog smells of onions?
A hot dog.

Ding dong bell,
Pussy's down the well,
But we've put some disinfectant down
And don't mind about the smell.

What do witches' cats strive for?
Purr-fection.

What do you call a witch's cat who can spring from the ground to her mistress's hat in one leap?
A good jum-purr.

Knock knock.
Who's there?
Josette.
Josette who?
Josette down and be quiet while I'm
    talking.

Knock knock.
Who's there?
Juan.
Juan who?
Juance upon a time there were
    three bears . . .

Knock knock.
Who's there?
Juan.
Juan who?
Just Juan of those things.

Knock knock.
Who's there?
Juana.
Juana who?
Juana go out with me?

Knock knock.
Who's there?
Juanita.
Juanita who?
Juanita big meal?

What lies on the ground 100 feet up in the air and smells?
A dead centipede.

What do you call a witch's cat who can do spells as well as her mistress?
An ex-purr-t.

☆　　☆　　☆

What's a vampire's favorite animal?
A giraffe.

☆　　☆　　☆

What do you get if you cross a werewolf with a frog?
A creature that can bite you from the other side of the road.

☆　　☆　　☆

What do you call a skeleton snake?
A rattler.

☆　　☆　　☆

What do you get if you cross a werewolf with a hyena?
I don't know but if it laughs, I'll join in.

☆　　☆　　☆

What kind of ant is good at adding up?
An account-ant.

☆　　☆　　☆

What medicine do you give a sick ant?
Antibiotics.

☆　　☆　　☆

Who is the most royal ant?
Princess Ant.

☆　　☆　　☆

What do you call an ant with five pairs of eyes?
Ant-ten-eye.

☆   ☆   ☆

Keeping Pet Snakes – by Sir Pent.

☆   ☆   ☆

Why did the ant-elope?
Nobody gnu.

☆   ☆   ☆

Who is the biggest gangster in the sea?
Al Caprawn.

What's worse than ants in your pants?
A bat in your bra.

☆   ☆   ☆

What kind of ant can you color with?
A cray-ant.

☆   ☆   ☆

What is Smokey the Elephant's middle name?
The.

☆   ☆   ☆

What do you call an ant who can't play the piano?
Discord-ant.

☆   ☆   ☆

What do you get if you cross an ant with half a pair of panties?
Pant.

☆   ☆   ☆

Knock knock.
Who's there?
Julie.
Julie who?
Julie'n on this door a lot?

☆   ☆   ☆

Knock knock.
Who's there?
Juliet.
Juliet who?
Juliet him get away with that?

☆   ☆   ☆

Knock knock.
Who's there?
Juliet.
Juliet who?
Juliet so much she burst!

☆   ☆   ☆

Knock knock.
Who's there?
July.
July who?
July or do you tell the truth?

☆   ☆   ☆

Knock knock.
Who's there?
June.
June who?
Juneno what time it is?

☆   ☆   ☆

What do you call an ant that likes to be alone?
An Independ-ant.

What do you call an ant with frog's legs?
An ant-phibian.

If ants are such busy insects, how come they find the time to turn up to picnics?

What do you call a hundred-year-old ant?
An antique.

Why don't anteaters get sick?
Because they're full of anty-bodies!

What's the biggest ant in the world?
An eleph-ant.
What is even bigger than that?
A gi-ant.

Why was the mother flea feeling down in the dumps?
Because she thought her children were all going to the dogs.

How do fleas travel?
Itch hiking.

What's the fastest thing in water?
A motor-pike.

Who was the most famous French ant?
Napoleant.

Who rides a dog and was a Confederate general during the American Civil War?
Robert E. Flea.

What did one flea say to another after a night out?
"Shall we walk home or take a dog?"

If a flea and a fly pass each other, what time is it?
Fly past flea.

What do you call a cheerful flea?
A hop-timist.

"Bring me a crocodile sandwich immediately."
"I'll make it snappy, sir."

Two fleas were running across the top of a packet of soap powder. "Why are we running so fast?" gasped one. "Because it says 'Tear Along the Dotted Line,'" replied the other.

What's the difference between a flea-bitten dog and a bored visitor?
One's going to itch. The other's itching to go.

Knock knock.
Who's there?
Karen.
Karen who?
Karen the can for you.

Knock knock.
Who's there?
Katherine.
Katherine who?
Katherine together for a social
    evening.

Knock knock.
Who's there?
Kathy.
Kathy who?
Kathy you again?

Knock knock.
Who's there?
Keanu.
Keanu who?
Keanu let me in? It's cold out here.

Knock knock.
Who's there?
Keith.
Keith who?
Keith your hands off me!

Why was the young kangaroo thrown out by his mother?
For smoking in bed.

What insect runs away from everything?
A flee.

A mother moth was telling her baby moth off saying, "If you don't eat all your cotton, you won't get any satin."

"Won't you let me live one of my own lives?" said the put-upon young cat to its parents.

What are the most faithful insects on the planet?
Fleas. Once they find someone they like they stick to them.

One goldfish to his tankmate: "If there's no God, who changes the water?"

There was once a puppy called May who loved to pick quarrels with animals who were bigger than she was. One day she argued with a lion. The next day was the first of June. Why?
Because that was the end of May!

"It's cruel," said the papa bear to his family on seeing a carload of humans, "to keep them caged up like that."

A big-mouthed, green, warty toad lived in a slimy swamp. He was a very friendly toad and enjoyed meeting other creatures in the swamp. One day he met a two-headed python.

"Hello, what are you?" he asked.

"I'm a two-headed python," replied the snake.

"Great! I'm a big-mouthed, green, warty toad – good to meet you!"

Then the next day he met a big, ugly warthog. "Hello, what are you?" he asked.

"I'm a big, ugly warthog," replied the warthog.

"I'm a big-mouthed, green warty toad – pleased to meet you!" said the toad.

Then just the next day he met a huge, furry Yeti. "Hello, what are you?" he asked.

"I'm a huge, furry Yeti and I eat big-mouthed, green warty toads," said the creature.

The toad pursed his lips together very small and whispered, "Hmm, you don't see many of those around do you?"

Just before the Ark set sail, Noah saw his two sons fishing over the side.

"Go easy on the bait, lads," he said. "Remember I've only got two worms."

☆   ☆   ☆

"Mommy," said the little lamb, "can I go to an all-ram's school when I'm five?"

"Don't be silly, darling," said his mother who was a very aristocratic sheep. "That would be frightfully non-U."

☆   ☆   ☆

"What's your new dog's name?"
"Dunno – he won't tell me."

Knock knock.
Who's there?
Kipper.
Kipper who?
Kipper your hands to yourself.

Knock knock.
Who's there?
Kismet.
Kismet who?
Kismet quick!

Knock knock.
Who's there?
Knee.
Knee who?
Kneed you ask?

Knock knock.
Who's there?
Kiwi.
Kiwi who?
Kiwit any longer.

Knock knock.
Who's there?
Knees.
Knees who?
Knees you every day.

What did the black cat do when its tail was cut off?
It went to a re-tail store.

☆ ☆ ☆

What do you get if you cross a hedgehog with a giraffe?
A long-necked toothbrush.

☆ ☆ ☆

What did the beaver say to the tree?
It sure is good to gnaw you.

☆ ☆ ☆

What's the difference between a coyote and a flea?
One howls on the prairie, and the other prowls on the hairy.

☆ ☆ ☆

What do you get if you cross a man-eating monster with a skunk?
A very ugly smell.

☆ ☆ ☆

Igor: Only this morning Dr Frankenstein completed another amazing operation. He crossed an ostrich with a centipede.
Dracula: And what did he get?
Igor: We don't know – we haven't managed to catch it yet.

☆ ☆ ☆

What do you get if you cross a sheepdog and a bunch of daisies?
Collie-flowers!

☆ ☆ ☆

First Cat: How did you get on in the milk-drinking contest?
Second Cat: Oh, I won by six laps!

"What's the difference between a kangaroo, a lumberjack and a bag of peanuts?"
"A kangaroo hops and chews and a lumberjack chops and hews."
"Yes, but what's the bag of peanuts for?"
"For monkeys like you."

What do you get if you cross a cow and a camel?
Lumpy milkshakes.

☆　☆　☆

Why don't centipedes play soccer?
Because by the time they've got their boots on it's time to go home.

☆　☆　☆

What do you get if you cross a sheep and a rainstorm?
A wet blanket.

☆　☆　☆

First Lion: Every time I eat a priest, I feel sick.
Second Lion: I know. It's hard to keep a good man down.

What do you get if you cross an elephant and peanut butter?
Either peanut butter that never forgets, or an elephant that sticks to the roof of your mouth.

☆　☆　☆

What do you get if you cross a zebra and a donkey?
A zeedonk.

☆　☆　☆

Knock knock.
Who's there?
Lara.
Lara who?
Lara lara laffs in Liverpool.

Knock knock.
Who's there?
Lacey.
Lacey who?
Lacey crazy days.

Knock knock.
Who's there?
Larry.
Larry who?
Larry up.

Knock knock.
Who's there?
Lana.
Lana who?
Lana the free.

Knock knock.
Who's there?
Larva.
Larva who?
Larva cup of coffee.

An elephant ran away from a circus and ended up in a little old lady's back garden. Now she had never seen an elephant before, so she rang the police. "Please come quickly," she said to the policeman who answered the phone. "There's a strange looking animal in my garden picking up cabbages with its tail."

"What's it doing with them?" asked the policeman.

"If I told you," said the old lady, "you'd never believe me!"

☆   ☆   ☆

What's a cow's favorite love song?
'When I Fall In Love, It Will Be For Heifer.'

Three animals were having a drink in a café, when the owner asked for the money. "I'm not paying," said the duck. "I've only got one bill and I'm not breaking it."

"I've spent my last buck," said the deer.

"Then the duck'll have to pay," said the skunk. "Getting here cost me my last scent."

☆   ☆   ☆

What fish do dogs chase?
Catfish.

☆   ☆   ☆

What's black and white, pongs and hangs from a line?
A drip-dry skunk.

☆   ☆   ☆

What's wet, smells and goes ba-bump, ba-bump?
A skunk in a spin-drier.

☆   ☆   ☆

A blind man was waiting to cross the road when a dog stopped and cocked its leg against him. The blind man felt in his pocket for a candy, bent down, and offered it to the dog. A passer-by remarked what a very kind act that was considering what the dog had done. "Not at all," said the blind man. "I only wanted to find out which end to kick."

☆　☆　☆

What do you get if you cross a nun and a chicken?
A pecking order.

☆　☆　☆

A man with a newt on his shoulder walked into a bar.
"What do you call him," asked the bartender.
"Tiny," said the man.
"Why do you call him Tiny?"
"Because he's my newt!"

☆　☆　☆

Did you hear about the snake with a bad cold?
No! Tell me about the snake with a bad cold.
She had to viper nose.

☆　☆　☆

What did the grape do when the elephant sat on it?
It let out a little wine.

"Gosh, it's raining cats and dogs," said Suzie looking out of the kitchen window.
"I know," said her mother who had just come in. "I've just stepped in a poodle!"

☆　☆　☆

Knock knock.
Who's there?
Leon.
Leon who?
Leon me – I'll support you.

Knock knock.
Who's there?
Leonie.
Leonie who?
Leonie one I love.

Knock knock.
Who's there?
Les.
Les who?
Les see what we can do.

Knock knock.
Who's there?
Leslie.
Leslie who?
Leslie town now before they catch us.

Knock knock.
Who's there?
Lester.
Lester who?
Lester we forget.

What do you call a flea that lives in an idiot's ear?

A space invader.

Why did the woman take a load of hay to bed?

To feed her nightmare.

Commissioned by a zoo to bring them some baboons, the big game hunter devised a novel scheme to trap them – his only requirements being a sack, a gun, and a particularly vicious and bad-tempered dog. He tramped into the jungle with his assistant, and after several weeks they finally reached an area where the baboons lived. "This is what we'll do," he explained to his baffled assistant. "I'll climb this tree and shake the branches; if there are any baboons up there, they will fall to the ground – and the dogs will bite their tails and immobilize them so that you can pick them up quite safely and put them in the sack."

"But what do I need the gun for?" asked the assistant.

"If I should fall out of the tree by mistake, shoot the dog."

What's black and white and noisy?

A zebra with a drum kit.

What do you get if you cross an eagle with a skunk?

A bird that stinks to high heaven.

217

Would you like a duck egg for tea?
Only if you quack it for me.

A man buying a camel was advised that to make it walk he should say "Few!", to make it run he should say "Many!", and to make it stop he should say "Amen!" On his first ride all went well. "Few!" he called, and off the camel went. "Many!" he shouted, and the camel began to run – straight for the edge of a cliff. But the new owner had forgotten the word to make the animal stop! As the cliff edge came closer he cried out in terror. "Lord save me! Lord save me! Amen!" And of course the camel stopped – right on the edge of the fearsome precipice. Whereupon the rider mopped his brow in relief and said, "Phew, that was clo- AAAAGH!"

What comes after cheese?
A mouse.

What do we get from naughty cows?
Bad milk!

A huge lion was roaring through the jungle when he suddenly saw a tiny mouse. He stopped and snarled at it menacingly. "You're very small," he growled fiercely.
"Well, I've been ill," replied the mouse piteously.

"My dog plays chess."
"Your dog plays chess? He must be really clever!"
"Oh, I don't know. I usually beat him three times out of four."

Knock knock.
Who's there?
Lisbon.
Lisbon who?
Lisbon away a long time.

Knock knock.
Who's there?
Little old lady.
Little old lady who?
I didn't know you could yodel.

☆　　☆　　☆

Knock knock.
Who's there?
Lionel.
Lionel who?
Lionel roar if you stand on its tail.

☆　　☆　　☆

Knock knock.
Who's there?
Liz.
Liz who?
Lizen carefully, I will say this only
    once.

☆　　☆　　☆

Knock knock.
Who's there?
Lisa.
Lisa who?
Lisa'n life.

What do you get if you cross a Scottish legend and a bad egg? The Loch Ness pongster.

Rabbits can multiply – but only a snake can be an adder.

"My budgie lays square eggs."
"That's amazing! Can it talk as well?"
"Yes, but only one word."
"What's that?"
"Ouch!"

If twenty dogs run after one dog, what time is it?
Twenty after one.

A man standing at a bus stop was eating a burger and fries. Next to him stood a lady with her little dog, which became very excited at the smell of the man's supper and began whining and jumping up at him. "Do you mind if I throw him a little?" said the man to the lady.
"Not at all," she replied, whereupon the man picked the dog up and threw it over a wall.

"Would you like to play with our new dog?"
"He looks very fierce. Does he bite?"
"That's what I want to find out."

"I'd like to buy a dog."
"Certainly, sir. Any particular breed? A Red Setter, perhaps?"
"No, not a Red Setter."
"A Golden Labrador?"
"No, not a Golden Labrador. I don't want a colored dog, just a black and white one."
"Why a black and white one, sir?"
"Isn't the license cheaper?"

How can you tell if an elephant has been sleeping in your bed?
The sheets are wrinkled and the bed smells of peanuts.

"Have you ever seen a man-eating tiger?"
"No, but in the café next door I once saw a man eating chicken!"

A man went into a pet store to buy a parrot. He was shown an especially fine one which he liked the look of, but he was puzzled by the two strings which were tied to its feet. "What are they for?" he asked the pet store manager.
"Ah well, sir," came the reply, "that's a very unusual feature of this particular parrot. You see, he's a trained parrot, sir – he used to be in the circus. If you pull the string on his left foot he says 'Hello' and if you pull the string on his right foot he says 'Goodbye.'"
"And what happens if you pull both strings at once?"
"I fall off my perch, you fool!" screeched the parrot.

Knock knock.
Who's there?
Lotte.
Lotte who?
Lotte sense.

Knock knock.
Who's there?
Lou.
Lou who?
Lou's your money on the horses.

Knock knock.
Who's there?
Louise.
Louise who?
Louise coming to tea today.

Knock knock.
Who's there?
Lucetta.
Lucetta who?
Lucetta a difficult problem.

Knock knock.
Who's there?
Lucille.
Lucille who?
Lucille-ing is dangerous to live
   under.

Why are skunks always arguing?
Cos they like to raise a stink.

"This loaf is nice and warm!"
"It should be – the cat's been sitting on it all day!"

How does an elephant go up a tree?
It stands on an acorn and waits for it to grow.

How do you milk a mouse?
You can't – the bucket won't fit under it.

☆   ☆   ☆

What is cowhide most used for?
Holding cows together.

☆   ☆   ☆

Why do bears wear fur coats?
They'd look silly in plastic macs.

What did the spider say to the beetle?
"Stop bugging me."

There were two tomatoes on horseback. Which was the cowboy?
Neither, they were both redskins.

There were ten zebras in the zoo. All but nine escaped. How many were left?
Nine!

A man who bought a dog took it back, complaining that it made a mess all over the house. "I thought you said it was housebroken," he moaned.
"So it is," said the previous owner. "It won't go anywhere else."

Did you hear about the man who took his pet skunk to the cinema? During a break in the movie, the woman sitting in front, who had been most affected by the animal's smell, turned round and said in a very sarcastic voice, "I'm surprised that an animal like that should appreciate a movie like this."
"So am I," said the man. "He hated the book."

A large sailing ship was at anchor off the coast of Mauritius, and two dodos watched the sailors rowing ashore.
"We'd better hide," said the first dodo.
"Why?" asked the second.
"Because," said the first, "we're supposed to be extinct, silly!"

Why can't dogs dance?
Because they've got two left feet.

Knock knock.
Who's there?
Lucinda.
Lucinda who?
(sing) "Lucinda sky with
    diamonds . . ."

☆   ☆   ☆

Knock knock.
Who's there?
Lucy.
Lucy who?
Lucylastic can let you down.

☆   ☆   ☆

Knock knock.
Who's there?
Lulu.
Lulu who?
Lulu's not working, can I use yours?

☆   ☆   ☆

Knock knock.
Who's there?
Luke.
Luke who?
Luke through the peephole and
    you'll see.

☆   ☆   ☆

Knock knock.
Who's there?
Lumley.
Lumley who?
Lumley cakes!

☆   ☆   ☆

A family of tortoises went into a café for some ice cream. They sat down and were about to start when Father Tortoise said, "I think it's going to rain, Junior, will you pop home and fetch my umbrella?" So off went Junior for Father's umbrella, but three days later he still hadn't returned.

"I think, dear," said Mother Tortoise to Father Tortoise, "that we had better eat Junior's ice cream before it melts." And a voice from the door said, "If you do that I won't go."

Father: Children! How many times must I remind you of your table manners! You're just like pigs! Children: That's because we're the children of an old bore.

Why does an ostrich have such a long neck?
Because its head is so far from its body.

What do you get if you cross a cow with a mule?
Milk with a kick in it.

☆   ☆   ☆

Sign in store window:
For Sale: Pedigree bulldog. Housebroken. Eats anything. Very fond of children.

☆   ☆   ☆

Good news! I've been given a goldfish for my birthday . . . the bad news is that I don't get the bowl until my next birthday!

☆   ☆   ☆

If a dog is tied to a rope 15 feet long, how can it reach a bone 30 feet away?
The rope isn't tied to anything!

A group of Chinese tourists who were on safari in Africa came across a pride of lions. "Oh look," said one of the lions. "A Chinese takeaway."

Why did the elephant cross the road?
To pick up the flattened chicken.

"When times were hard, a family of New York pigeons moved to the top of the Empire State Building and every morning and every evening the family left the roost, flew around the top of the building and let their droppings fall on to the street hundreds of feet below."
"I'm not sure I get the point of this story."
"Well, in hard times, you have to make a little go a long way!"

The eighth Earl of Jerry was showing Americans round his ancestral home, Jerry Hall, when one of them pointed to a moth-eaten, stuffed polar bear. "Gee! That beast sure smells," said the American. "Why d'ya keep it?"
"For sentimental reasons," replied the Earl. "It was shot by my mother when she and my father were on a trip to the Arctic."
"What's it stuffed with?" asked the American.
"The seventh Earl of Jerry!"

Knock knock.
Who's there?
Madonna.
Madonna who?
Madonna's being mean – tell her
    off!

Knock knock.
Who's there?
Madrid.
Madrid who?
Madrid you wash my sports kit?

Knock knock.
Who's there?
Mae.
Mae who?
(sing) "Mae be it's because I'm a
    Londoner."

Knock knock.
Who's there?
Maggot.
Maggot who?
Maggot me this new dress today.

Knock knock.
Who's there?
Maia.
Maia who?
Maianimals are like children to me.

Why do elephants have flat feet?
From jumping out of tall trees.

What do you get if you cross a
chicken with a cow?
Roost beef.

What do you get if you cross a flea
with a rabbit?
Bugs Bunny.

What do you get if you cross a
crocodile with a flower?
I don't know, but I'm not going to smell
it.

What did the dragon say when he saw
St George in his shining armor?
"Oh no, not more canned food."

What do you call a multi-story pig-
pen?
A styscraper.

What smells of fish and goes round
and round at 100 miles an hour?
A goldfish in a blender.

Is the squirt from an elephant's trunk
very powerful?
Of course – a jumbo jet can keep
500 people in the air for hours at a
time.

"Why are you crying, little boy?"
"Cos we've just had to have our dog
put down!" sobbed the lad.
"Was he mad?"
"Well he wasn't too happy about it."

Did you hear about the baby skunk
who asked his mother if he could
have a chemistry set for Christmas?
She wouldn't let him have one in case
he stank the house out.

Why did the pig run away from the
pig-pen?
He felt that the other pigs were
taking him for grunted.

"Can I have another slice of lemon?"
a man in a bar asked the bartender.
"We don't have any lemons in this
bar!"
"Oh no!" said the man. "If that's true,
I've just squeezed your canary into my
gin and tonic!"

Knock knock.
Who's there?
Mao.
Mao who?
Maothful of toffee.

Knock knock.
Who's there?
March.
March who?
March, march, quick, quick, march.

Knock knock.
Who's there?
Marcia.
Marcia who?
Marcia me!

☆　☆　☆

Knock knock.
Who's there?
Manchu.
Manchu who?
Manchu your food six times.

Knock knock.
Who's there?
Mandy.
Mandy who?
Mandy guns.

What's the difference between a wild camel and a bully?
One's a big, smelly, bad-tempered beast and the other is an animal.

How do you make an elephant sandwich?
First of all you get a very large loaf . . .

What's green and smells?
Kermit's nose.

What do you call pigs who live together?
Pen-pals.

Is it true that carrots are good for the eyesight?
Well you never see rabbits wearing glasses.

What do you get if you cross a chicken with an octopus?
A Sunday dinner where everybody gets a leg.

232

Charlie: I'd like to talk to you in kangaroo-speak.
Clare: What would you say?
Charlie: Hop it!

Aggie: I've made the chicken soup.
Maggie: Thank goodness! I thought it was for us!

What's purple and barks at people?
A grape dane.

What's an Australian animal's favorite game?
Mortal Wombat.

What's yellow and sweet and holds baby monkeys?
An Ape-ricot.

What keys are furry?
Monkeys.

Knock knock.
Who's there?
Marie.
Marie who?
Marie for love.

Knock knock.
Who's there?
Marietta.
Marietta who?
Marietta whole loaf!

Knock knock.
Who's there?
Marilyn.
Marilyn who?
Marilyn, she'll make you a good
   wife.

Knock knock.
Who's there?
Marion.
Marion who?
Marion idiot and repent at leisure.

Knock knock.
Who's there?
Mark.
Mark who?
Mark my words.

Two elderly teachers were talking over old times and saying how much things had changed. "I mean," said the first, "I caught one of the boys kissing one of the girls yesterday." "Extraordinary," said the second. "I didn't even kiss my wife before I married her, did you?" "I can't remember. What was her maiden name?"

☆　☆　☆

Freda: Boys whisper they love me.
Fred: Well, they wouldn't admit it out loud, would they?

Flash Harry gave his girlfriend a mink stole for her birthday.
Well, it may not have been mink, but it's fairly certain it was stole.

☆　☆　☆

When my girlfriend goes out riding, she looks like part of the horse.
When she dismounts, she still looks like part of the horse.

☆　☆　☆

One day Tony's girlfriend wrote to him to say their friendship was off and could she have her photograph back? Tony sent her a pile of pictures of different girls with the message, "I can't remember what you look like. Could you please take out your photo and return the rest?"

☆　☆　☆

Why did the science teacher marry the school cleaner?
Because she swept him off his feet.

My boyfriend is such an idiot. The other day I saw him hitting himself on the head with a hammer. He was trying to make his head swell so his hat wouldn't fall over his eyes.

The french mistress had broken off her engagement. The science mistress asked her what had happened and said, "I thought it was love at first sight."
"It was," replied the french mistress "but it was the second and third sights that changed my mind."

My girlfriend thinks I'm a great wit. Well, she's half right.

Simon: My girlfriend and I fell out last night. She wanted to go and watch ice-skating, but I wanted to go to the football game.
Peter: What was the ice-skating like?

Jamie: Is your new girlfriend good-looking?
Hamish: Yes, except for her pedestrian eyes.
Jamie: What are pedestrian eyes?
Hamish: They look both ways before they cross.

Knock knock.
Who's there?
Maude.
Maude who?
Mauden my job's worth.

☆　　☆　　☆

Knock knock.
Who's there?
Mauve.
Mauve who?
Mauve over!

☆　　☆　　☆

Knock knock.
Who's there?
Maude.
Maude who?
Maude of wood.

☆　　☆　　☆

Knock knock.
Who's there?
Mavis.
Mavis who?
Mavis be the best day of your life.

☆　　☆　　☆

Knock knock.
Who's there?
Maude.
Maude who?
Mauden living.

☆　　☆　　☆

What did the two acrobats say when they got married?
We're head over heels in love!

What did the undertaker say to his girlfriend?
Em-balmy about you.

☆　☆　☆

Ben's new girlfriend uses such greasy lipstick that he has to sprinkle his face with sand to get a better grip.

☆　☆　☆

Anne: Ugh! The water in my glass is cloudy.
Dan, trying to impress his new girlfriend: It's all right, it's just the glass that hasn't been washed.

☆　☆　☆

A horrible old witch surprised all her friends by announcing that she was going to get married.
"But," said another old hag, "you always said men were stupid. And you vowed never to marry."
"Yes, I know," said the witch. "But I finally found one who asked me."

She's the kind of girl that boys look at twice – they can't believe it the first time.

☆　　☆　　☆

Every time I take my girlfriend out for a meal she eats her head off.
She looks better that way.

☆　　☆　　☆

A man who forgets his wife's birthday is certain to get something to remember her by.

☆　　☆　　☆

My husband must be the meanest man in the world. He recently found a crutch – then he broke his leg so he could use it.

☆　　☆　　☆

My girlfriend is a beautiful redhead – no hair, just a red head.

☆　　☆　　☆

I can't understand why people say my girlfriend's legs look like matchsticks. They do look like sticks – but they certainly don't match.

Woman: If you were my husband I'd poison your coffee.
Man: And if you were my wife, I'd drink it.

☆　　☆　　☆

Did you hear about the girl who got engaged to a chap and then found out he had a wooden leg?
She broke it off, of course . . .

☆　　☆　　☆

Knock knock.
Who's there?
Maya.
Maya who?
Maya turn.

Knock knock.
Who's there?
McEnroe.
McEnroe who?
McEnroe fast with his own oar.

Knock knock.
Who's there?
Me.
Me who?
I didn't know you had a cat!

Knock knock.
Who's there?
Mecca.
Mecca who?
Mecca my day!

Knock knock.
Who's there?
Meg.
Meg who?
Meg a fuss.

A policeman discovered a suspicious-looking character lolling up against a doorway. "What are you doing here?" the officer demanded.

"I live here," said the man. "I've lost my front door key."

"Well, ring the bell, then," said the policeman.

"Oh, I did ten minutes ago."

"Perhaps there's no one in then," suggested the officer.

"Oh yes, my wife and two children are in."

"So why not ring again?"

"No," said the man, "let 'em wait."

A very shy young man went into an optometrist's one day to order a new pair of spectacles. Behind the counter was an extremely pretty young girl, which reduced the customer to total confusion. "Can I help you, sir?" she asked with a ravishing smile.

"Er . . . yes . . . er . . . I want a pair of rim-speckled hornicles . . . I mean I want a pair of heck-rimmed spornicles . . . er . . . I mean . . . At which point the optometrist himself came to the rescue.

"It's all right, Miss Jones. What the gentleman wants is a pair of rim-sporned hectacles."

☆　　☆　　☆

Yes, darling, I do like your dress – but isn't it a little early for Halloween?

"My Uncle Ben and Aunt Flo haven't had a row for five years."
"That's wonderful."
"Not really. Uncle Ben lives in China."

"I'm suffering from bad breath."
"You should do something about it!"
"I did. I just sent my wife to the dentist."

George had reached the age of 46, and not only was he still unmarried but he had never had a girlfriend.
"Come along now, George," said his father. "It's high time you got yourself a wife and settled down. Why, at your age I'd been married 20 years."
"But that was to Mom," said his son. "You can't expect me to marry a stranger!"

In the good old days, husbands used to come home from work, and say, "What's cooking?" Now they say, "What's thawing?"

"What's the matter?" one man asked another.
"My wife left me when I was in the bath last night," sobbed the second man.
"She must have been waiting for years for the chance," replied the first.

Knock knock.
Who's there?
Michael.
Michael who?
Michaelock has stopped ticking.

☆　　☆　　☆

Knock knock.
Who's there?
Michael.
Michael who?
Michael beat you up if you don't
　　open the door!

☆　　☆　　☆

Knock knock.
Who's there?
Michelle.
Michelle who?
Michelle has sounds of the sea in
　　it.

☆　　☆　　☆

Knock knock.
Who's there?
Mike.
Mike who?
Mike the best of it.

☆　　☆　　☆

Knock knock.
Who's there?
Mike.
Mike who?
Mike-andle's just blown out. It's all
　　dark.

☆　　☆　　☆

"My husband's just opened a store."

"Really? How's he doing?"

"Six months. He opened it with a crowbar."

Harry was madly in love with Betty, but couldn't pluck up enough courage to pop the question face to face. Finally he decided to ask her on the telephone. "Darling," he blurted out, "will you marry me?"

"Of course, I will, you silly boy," she replied. "Who is it speaking?"

"My Peter keeps telling everyone he's going to marry the most beautiful girl in the world."

"What a shame! And after all the time you've been engaged!"

Mrs Jones and her little daughter Karen were outside the church watching all the comings and goings of a wedding. After the photographs had been taken, everyone had driven off to the reception and all the excitement was over, Karen said to her mother, "Why did the bride change her mind, Mommy?"

"How do you mean, change her mind?" asked Mrs Jones.

"Well," said the moppet, "she went into the church with one man and came out with another."

"What's your new perfume called?" a young man asked his girlfriend.

"High Heaven," she replied.

"I asked what it was called, not what it smells to!"

"Why did you refuse to marry Richard, Tessa?"

"Cos he said he would die if I didn't and I'm just curious."

When Mr Maxwell's wife left him, he couldn't sleep.
She had taken the bed.

"But she's so young to get married," sobbed Diana's mother. "Only seventeen!"

"Try not to cry about it," said her husband soothingly. "Think of it not so much as losing a daughter but as gaining a bathroom."

"Is my dinner hot?" asked the excessively late husband.

"It should be," said his furious wife. "It's been on the fire since seven o'clock!"

A salesman was trying to persuade a housewife to buy a life insurance policy. "Just imagine if your husband were to die," he said. "What would you get?"

"Oh a sheepdog, I think," she replied. "They're so well behaved."

"Why do they call her an after-dinner speaker?"

"Because every time she speaks to a man she's after a dinner."

Knock knock.
Who's there?
Mike and Angelo.
Mike and Angelo who?
Mike and Angelo's David.

Knock knock.
Who's there?
Mikey.
Mikey who?
Mikey is stuck.

Knock knock.
Who's there?
Miles.
Miles who?
Miles away.

Knock knock.
Who's there?
Milo.
Milo who?
Milo bed is too uncomfortable.

Knock knock.
Who's there?
Mimi.
Mimi who?
Mimi b-bicycle's b-broken.

Knock knock.
Who's there?
Missouri.
Missouri who?
Missouri me! I'm so scared!

Knock knock.
Who's there?
Miss Piggy.
Miss Piggy who?
Miss Piggy went to market, Miss
    Piggy stayed at home . . .

Knock knock.
Who's there?
Money.
Money who?
Money is hurting – I knocked it
    playing football.

Knock knock.
Who's there?
Mom.
Mom who?
Mom's the word.

Knock knock.
Who's there?
Monster.
Monster who?
Monster munch.

Mr Brown: I hate to tell you, but your wife just fell in the wishing well.
Mr Smith: It works!

"Mommy, mommy, why do you keep poking daddy in the ribs?"
"If I don't, the fire will go out."

Romeo: You remind me of a movie star.
Juliet: Which one?
Romeo: Lassie.

"My husband really embarrassed me yesterday. We were at the vicarage for tea and he drank his with his little finger sticking out."
"But that's considered polite in some circles."
"Not with the tea bag hanging from it, it's not."

Harry: I've a soft spot for you.
Mary: Really?
Harry: Yes, in the middle of a bog!

James: I call my girlfriend Peach.
John: Because she's beautiful?
James: No, because she's got a heart of stone!

"What do you do?" a young man asked the beautiful girl he was dancing with.
"I'm a nurse."
"I wish I could be ill and let you nurse me," he whispered in her ear.
"That would be miraculous. I work on the maternity ward."

Knock knock.
Who's there?
Moses.
Moses who?
Moses the lawn.

Knock knock.
Who's there?
Mosquito.
Mosquito who?
Mosquito smoking soon.

Knock knock.
Who's there?
Morrissey.
Morrissey who?
Morrissey the pretty birdies?

Knock knock.
Who's there?
Moth.
Moth who?
Moth get mythelf a key.

Knock knock.
Who's there?
Moscow.
Moscow who?
Moscow home soon.

"Some girls think I'm handsome," said the young Romeo, "and some girls think I'm ugly. What do you think, Juliet?"
"A bit of both. Pretty ugly."

Two men were remembering their wedding days. "It was dreadful," said Albert. "I got the most terrible fright."
"What happened?" asked Algie.
"I married her," replied Albert.

Your sister's boyfriend certainly has staying power.
In fact, he never leaves.

Michael: It's hard for my girlfriend to eat.
Maureen: Why?
Michael: She can't bear to stop talking.

☆ ☆ ☆

Freddie had persuaded Amanda to marry him, and was formally asking her father for his permission. "Sir," he said, "I would like to have your daughter for my wife."
"Why can't she get one of her own?" said Amanda's father, disconcertingly.

"They say he has a leaning towards blondes."
"Yes, but they keep pushing him back."

"My sister's going out with David."
"Any girl who goes out with David must be able to appreciate the simpler things in life."

Bertie: You remind me of a Greek statue.
Gertie: Do you mean you think I'm beautiful?
Bertie: Yes, beautiful, but not all there.

My brother's looking for a wife. Trouble is, he can't find a woman who loves him as much as he loves himself.

On their first evening in their new home the bride went in to the kitchen to fix the drinks. Five minutes later she came back into the lounge in tears.
"What's the matter, my angel?" asked her husband anxiously.
"Oh, Derek!" she sobbed. "I put the ice cubes in hot water to wash them and they've disappeared!"

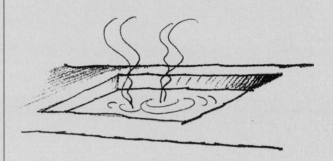

My boyfriend only has two faults – everything he says and everything he does!

"I hear she doesn't care for a man's company."
"Not unless he owns it."

251

Knock knock.
Who's there?
Mountain.
Mountain who?
Mountain debts.

Knock knock.
Who's there?
Mozart.
Mozart who?
Mozart is very beautiful.

Knock knock.
Who's there?
Muffin.
Muffin who?
Muffin to declare.

Knock knock.
Who's there?
Munich.
Munich who?
Munich some money for me?

Knock knock.
Who's there?
Munro.
Munro who?
Munro fast to the other side.

"Why aren't you married?"
"I was born that way."

New Wife: Will you love me when I'm old and fat and ugly?
New Husband: Of course I do!

Wife: I had to marry you to find out how stupid you are.
Husband: You should have known that the minute I asked you.

"I hear she's highly strung."
"She should be!"

"He bought her engagement ring from a famous millionaire."
"Woolworth?"

What's the best way to get rid of excess fat?
Divorce him.

Stan: You remind me of the sea.
Sue: Because I'm so wild and romantic?
Stan: No, because you make me sick!

"May I go swimming, Mommy?"
"No, you may not. There are sharks here."
"But Daddy's swimming."
"He's insured."

Why did the Ancient Egyptian girl start crying?
Because her dad just became a mummy.

Golfer: Have you packed all my golf gear in the car?
Wife: Yes, dear: clubs, map, compass, emergency rations . . .

What did the sad plumber say to his girlfriend?
"It's all over Flo!"

Why didn't the female frog lay eggs?
Because her husband spawned her affections.

Jack: I was chosen by a computer as being an ideal boyfriend.
John: A computer's about the only thing that would have you as a boyfriend.

Knock knock.
Who's there?
Nadia.
Nadia who?
Nadia head if you want to come in.

☆　　☆　　☆

Knock knock.
Who's there?
Nancy.
Nancy who?
Nancy a piece of cake?

☆　　☆　　☆

Knock knock.
Who's there?
Nanny.
Nanny who?
Nanny people are waiting to come
　　in.

☆　　☆　　☆

Knock knock.
Who's there?
Nanny.
Nanny who?
Nanny-one home?

☆　　☆　　☆

Knock knock.
Who's there?
Neil.
Neil who?
Neil down before the vampire king!

☆　　☆　　☆

"He's the kind of boy girls dream about."
"That's better than seeing him in broad daylight."

Mrs Brown was always complaining about her husband. "If things go on like this I'll have to leave him," she moaned to Mrs Jenkins.
"Give him the soft-soap treatment," said Mrs Jenkins.
"I tried that," replied Mrs Brown, "but it didn't work. He spotted it at the top of the stairs."

Inuit Girl: There's something I'd like to give you.
Inuit Boy: What?
Inuit Girl: The cold shoulder.

Wife: Did you like the food I cooked for you?
Husband: Let's just say it was a real swill dinner.

Girl: I never wear lipstick.
Boy: No, because you can't keep your mouth still for long enough to put it on!

"How are you getting on with James?"
"Well, he's a little dull until you get to know him."
"And when you have got to know him you'll find he's a real bore!"

Sheila: When I go out with John I feel like jumping for joy.
Stella: Do you? I feel like jumping off a bridge.

"He always has to have the last word."
"It wouldn't be so bad if it didn't take him so long to reach it."

Husband: You took me for better or worse.
Wife: Yes, but I didn't think it would be this much worse.

"He is pretty boring."
"Yes, but he does have occasional moments of silence."

Wife: We've been married 12 whole months.
Husband: Seems more like a year to me.

☆   ☆   ☆

Bill: What would it take to make you give me a kiss?
Gill: An anesthetic.

Knock knock.
Who's there?
Ninja.
Ninja who?
Ninja with me every day.

Knock knock.
Who's there?
Noah.
Noah who?
Noah counting for taste.

Knock knock.
Who's there?
Noah.
Noah who?
Noah don't know who you are either.

Knock knock.
Who's there?
Nobody.
Nobody who?
Just nobody.

Knock knock.
Who's there?
Noise.
Noise who?
Noise to see you.

Wife, to Husband: Boil the baby while I feed the potatoes, will you?

Saul: My wife worships me.
Paul: Why do you think that?
Saul: She puts burnt offerings in front of me three times a day.

Myron: I can marry anyone I please!
Byron: But you don't please anyone!

Wife: I've given you the best years of my life.
Husband: Are you asking me for a receipt?

Foreign Visitor: And is this your most charming wife?
Husband: No, she's the only one I've got.

Mrs Rose: Where are you going to?
Mrs Thorn: The doctor's. I don't like the look of my husband.
Mrs Rose: Can I come with you? I can't stand the sight of mine!

Brian: Why are you covered with scratches?

Byron: My girlfriend said it with flowers.

Brian: That sounds romantic.

Byron: It wasn't, she hit me round the head with a bunch of roses.

Guy: What did you buy your girlfriend for her birthday?

Cy: I got her a bottle of toilet water. It was very expensive.

Guy: You should have come round to our house. You could have had as much water as you wanted out of our toilet for free.

"Why do you call your girlfriend 'Treasure'?"

"Because I wonder where she was dug up!"

A man ran after a lady in the street, tapped her on the shoulder and said, "Hello, darling."

"Do I know you?" she asked coldly. The man was covered in confusion.

"Oh, please excuse me," he said. "I thought you were my wife. You look just like her behind."

Knock knock.
Who's there?
Nola.
Nola who?
Nolaner driver may drive a car
    alone.

Knock knock.
Who's there?
Norma.
Norma who?
Normally the butler opens the door.

Knock knock.
Who's there?
Norman.
Norman who?
Norman behavior is expected here!

Knock knock.
Who's there?
Norway.
Norway who?
Norway is this your house – it's so
    big!

Knock knock.
Who's there?
Nose.
Nose who?
Nosinging in the house.

"Why do you call your boyfriend 'Wonder'?"
"Because I look at him and wonder!"

Jackie: I hear John took you to one of the best restaurants in town.
Tackie: Yes, but he didn't take me in.

"I hear they're planning a runaway marriage."
"Yes, but every time she fixes it up he runs away!"

Billy: Since I met you I haven't been able to eat or drink.
Tilly: Because you love me so much?
Billy: No, because I'm broke.

Holly: How are you getting on with your advertisements for a husband? Have you had any replies?
Molly: Yes, lots. And they all say the same – take mine!

Barney: My girlfriend's cooking's like a good man.
Arnie: What do you mean?
Barney: Hard to keep down!

Wife: One more word from you and I'm going back to mother!
Husband: Taxi!

Sharon: Do you like me?
Darren: As girls go, you're fine. And the further you go the better.

Jill: Darling, whisper something soft and sweet in my ear.
Jack: Black forest cherry cake.

They say he fell in love with his wife the second time he met her. The first time he didn't know how rich she was.

Young Man: I've come to ask for your daughter's hand.
Father: You'll have to take the rest of her too or the deal's off.

Shona: My boyfriend says I'm beautiful.
Rhona: They do say love is blind.

Tilly: Who's that woman with the little wart?
Millie: Shh, he's her husband.

Knock knock.
Who's there?
Olive.
Olive who?
Olive in this house – what are you
   doing here?

Knock knock.
Who's there?
Oliver.
Oliver who?
Oliver lone and I'm frightened of
   monsters.

Knock knock.
Who's there?
Olivia.
Olivia who?
Olivia'l is great for cooking.

Knock knock.
Who's there?
Oliver.
Oliver who?
Oliver long way away.

Knock knock.
Who's there?
Olivier.
Olivier who?
Olivier all my money in my will.

Clark: I'm not rich like Arwin, and I don't have a country estate like Brian or a Ferrari like Clive, but I love you and I want to marry you.
Clara: I love you too, but what did you say about Brian?

☆　☆　☆

"My husband thinks he's a squirrel."
"I expect he's just another nut-case."

☆　☆　☆

Kerry: My girlfriend's different from all other girls.
Terry: I bet she's different. She's the only girl around who'll go out with you!

Peter: That man is the ugliest person I've ever seen!
Anita: He's my husband.
Peter: Oh dear, I'm so sorry.
Anita: You're sorry!

☆　☆　☆

They're a perfect couple – he works in a chip shop and there's something fishy about her.

☆　☆　☆

Hotel Porter: May I carry your bag, sir?
Hotel Guest: That won't be necessary, my wife is perfectly capable of walking.

☆　☆　☆

Nigel: Have you noticed how many girls don't want to get married nowadays?
Neil: No. How do you know?
Nigel: I've asked them all.

☆　☆　☆

"My wife thinks she's a door."
"Let me know when she's unhinged."

Bill: I've written you a poem, but you mustn't read it until after my death.
Gill: How wonderful! I can't wait to read it!

Husband: What would you do if I were dead and gone and couldn't pick the strawberries for you?
Wife: I'd buy frozen ones.

Mrs White: Do you miss your husband terribly now he's dead?
Mrs Black: Yes. I've had so many problems sorting out his estate I sometimes wish he were still alive!

Romeo: I'd go to the end of the earth for you.
Juliet: Good. And when you get there, jump off!

Mr Hedge: I say, old boy, you just shot my wife!
Mr Tree: So sorry, old lad, have a shot at mine!

Knock knock.

Who's there?

Omar.

Omar who?

Omar goodness, what are you doing
    in there?

☆   ☆   ☆

Knock knock.

Who's there?

Omelette.

Omelette who?

Omelette smarter than I look!

☆   ☆   ☆

Knock knock.

Who's there?

One-eye.

One-eye who?

You're the One-eye can't stand!

Knock knock.

Who's there?

Ooze.

Ooze who?

Ooze that knocking at my door?

☆   ☆   ☆

Bridegroom: Will you really be able to put up with me for the rest of your life?
Bride: Of course, dear, you'll be out at work most of the time!

First Man: Is your wife fat?
Second Man: Put it this way, when we were married and I carried her across the threshold, I had to make two trips.

Romeo: Will you come to the movies with me tonight?
Juliet: Oh, no, I never go out with perfect strangers.
Romeo: Who says I'm perfect?

"They say she's been asked to get married hundreds of times."
"Really? Who by?"
"Her parents!"

Knock, knock.
Who's there?
Onya.
Onya who?
Onya marks, get set, go.

After a visit to the circus, Geoff and Don were discussing the thrills and marvels they had seen.
"I didn't think much of the knife-thrower. Did you?" said Geoff.
"I thought he was great!" enthused Don.
"Well I didn't," said Geoff. "He kept chucking those knives at that soppy girl but he didn't hit her once!"

"If we get married do you think you'll be able to live on my income?"
"Of course. But what will you live on?"

Gillie: Did the bride look beautiful?
Millie: She wore a lovely dress. I wonder when that style will be in fashion again?

Judge: Your first three wives died from eating poisonous mushrooms, and now your fourth wife has drowned in your swimming pool. Isn't that all a little odd?

Prisoner: Not really. She didn't like mushrooms.

"Are they happily married?"

"Oh, yes. She's happy and he's married."

Wife: Today we're having Chicken Surprise.

Husband: What's the surprise?

Wife: You're cooking it.

Harry: Is your girlfriend conceited?

Larry: I think so. She only looks at me so she can see her reflection in my glasses.

☆   ☆   ☆

"My wife says that if I don't give up golf she'll leave me."

"Say, that's tough, old man."

"Yeah, I'm going to miss her."

☆   ☆   ☆

When my mom and dad got engaged she asked him if he would be giving her a ring. He said, "Of course. What's your number?"

☆   ☆   ☆

Boss: You're looking much better now, Reynolds. How's that pain?

Reynolds: She's away on a business trip.

☆   ☆   ☆

Knock knock.
Who's there?
Opi.
Opi who?
Opi cushion.

☆　☆　☆

Knock knock.
Who's there?
Orange.
Orange who?
Orange your day to suit the
　weather.

Knock knock.
Who's there?
Organ.
Organ who?
Organize a party – it's my birthday.

☆　☆　☆

Knock knock.
Who's there?
Orson.
Orson who?
Orson, let your daddy in.

☆　☆　☆

Knock knock.
Who's there?
Oscar.
Oscar who?
Oscar foolish question, get a foolish
　answer.

☆　☆　☆

Juliet: Whisper those three little words that will make my day.
Romeo: Go to hell!

Wife: The hospital can't do my operation yet, there isn't a bed available.
Husband: Oh dear. That means you'll have to go on talking about your previous operation for a bit longer.

"My husband's a millionaire."
"He was a multi-millionaire before you married him."

Mr Black: I took my wife to the beauty parlor yesterday and I had to sit and wait all afternoon for her.
Mr White: Whatever was she having done?
Mr Black: Nothing – she just went for an estimate.

Katie: Are you still looking for a husband?
Kathy: Yes.
Katie: What's the problem?
Kathy: I can't find anyone clever enough to make a lot of money and daft enough to spend it all on me.

Jim: So what happened when you sent your photo to that woman who advertised in the Lonely Hearts column?
Kim: She sent it back saying she wasn't that lonely.

She's been married to so many rich men and then divorced she must have got richer by decrees.

Romeo: If you won't marry me I'll hang myself from that tree in front of your house.
Juliet: Please don't. You know Father doesn't like young men hanging around in front of the house!

"My wife is very dear to me."
"Yes, I believe she costs you a fortune."

At a very posh wedding, one of the guests broke wind. The bridegroom was furious and rounded on the guilty party. "How dare you break wind in front of my wife?" he roared.
"Sorry," said the guest. "Was it her turn?"

"Some husbands can cook, but don't."
"My husband can't cook, but does."

☆ ☆ ☆

She talks so much he's never on speaking terms with her, just listening terms!

☆ ☆ ☆

"Can your husband cook?"
"Let's just say that yesterday he burned the salad."

Knock knock.
Who's there?
Pammy.
Pammy who?
Pammy something nice when you
   are at the shops!

☆　　☆　　☆

Knock knock.
Who's there?
Panon.
Panon who?
Panon my intrusion.

☆　　☆　　☆

Knock knock.
Who's there?
Panther.
Panther who?
Panther what you wear on your
   legth.

☆　　☆　　☆

Knock knock.
Who's there?
Pablo.
Pablo who?
Pablo the candles out.

☆　　☆　　☆

Knock knock.
Who's there?
Pam.
Pam who?
Pamper yourself.

☆　　☆　　☆

Wife: Did you really marry me because you'd heard my uncle had left me a fortune?
Husband: No, I'd have married you no matter who had left you a fortune.

"You can always spot my wife at a party."
"How?"
"Look for two people talking. If one of them looks bored, the other is my wife."

"They say he's her idol."
"He certainly never does anything."

Giles: Can you lend me 10 cents? I want to phone a girlfriend.
Miles: Here's 25 cents. Phone all your girlfriends.

Darren: I'm afraid I've lost all my money.
Sharon: Oh dear, what a shame. I'll really miss you.

"When he told me he loved me he said he'd go through anything for me."
"And has he?"
"So far he's only gone through my bank account."

"Doctor, doctor, my husband thinks he is a piece of chewing gum."
"Well send him to see me."
"I can't – he's stuck under the table."

A fat girl went into a café and ordered two slices of apple pie with four scoops of ice cream covered with lashings of raspberry sauce and piles of chopped nuts.

"Would you like a cherry on the top?" asked the waitress.

"No thanks," said the girl, "I'm on a diet."

Who are some of the werewolves' cousins?
The whatwolves and the whenwolves.

What happened at the outlaws' party?
The chief outlaw's mother-in-law turned up because she thought it was an in-laws party.

Knock, Knock
Who's there?
Anita Loos.
Anita Loos who?
Anita Loos about 20 pounds.

☆   ☆   ☆

Boy: What's the biggest ant in the world?
Girl: My aunt Fatima.
Boy: No it's an elephant.
Girl: You obviously haven't met my aunt Fatima.

Knock knock.
Who's there?
Pasta.
Pasta who?
Pasta salt please.

Knock knock.
Who's there?
Pastille.
Pastille who?
Pastille long road you'll find a
    village.

Knock knock.
Who's there?
Patrick.
Patrick who?
Patricked me into coming.

Knock knock.
Who's there?
Patty.
Patty who?
Patty-cake.

Knock knock.
Who's there?
Paul.
Paul who?
Paul up a chair and I'll tell you.

Beautician: Did that mud pack I gave you for your wife improve her appearance?
Man: It did for a while – then it fell off.

Mother: John, why did you put a slug in auntie's bed?
John: Because I couldn't find a snake.

Boy: Grandpa, do you know how to croak?
Grandpa: No, I don't think so. Why?
Boy: Because daddy says he'll be a rich man when you do.

First Boy: My dad saw a horrible witch and didn't turn a hair!
Second Boy: I'm not surprised – your dad's bald!

My sister is so dim she thinks that a cartoon is a song you sing in a car.

That's nothing: my sister thinks that a juggernaut is an empty beer mug.

Older Brother: When I was a sailor I sailed both ways across the Atlantic without taking a bath.
Younger Brother: I always said you were a dirty double crosser!

Did you hear about the witch who was so ugly, at night she put her whole body up in curlers.

What's big and red and lies upside down in a gutter?
A dead bus.

First Witch: What's your new boyfriend like?
Second witch: He's mean, nasty, ugly, smelly, and totally evil – but he has some bad points too.

Witch: Have you ever seen someone who looked like me before?
Girl: Yes, but I had to pay admission.

Look at that bald man over there. It's the first time I've seen a parting with ears.

Knock knock.
Who's there?
Pecan.
Pecan who?
Pecan work it out.

☆   ☆   ☆

Knock knock.
Who's there?
Pecan.
Pecan who?
Pecan somebody your own size.

Knock knock.
Who's there?
Peg.
Peg who?
Peg your pardon, I've got the wrong
    door.

☆   ☆   ☆

Knock knock.
Who's there?
Pen.
Pen who?
Pent-up emotions!

☆   ☆   ☆

Knock knock.
Who's there?
Pencil.
Pencil who?
Pencil fall down if your belt snaps.

☆   ☆   ☆

Millie: You've got a Roman nose.
Tilly: Like Julius Caesar?
Millie: No, it's roamin' all over your face.

A little man walked into a police station one day and said, "I've got three big brothers and we all live in the same room. My eldest brother has seven cats. Another one has three dogs, and the third has a goat. I want you to do something about the smell."
"Are there windows in your room?" asked the duty officer.
"Yes, of course there are!" said the man.
"Have you tried opening them?"
"What, and lose all my pigeons?"

Monster: What's the matter, son?
Boy: The boy next door says I look just like you.
Monster: What did you say?
Boy: Nothing, he's bigger than me.

What did the Speak-Your-Weight machine say when the fat lady stepped on?
One at a time, please.

Did you hear about the witch who was ashamed of her long black hair?
She always wore long gloves to cover it up.

Did you hear about the witch who did a four-year course in ugliness? She finished it in two.

Did you hear about the witch who went in for the "lovely legs" competition? She was beaten by the microphone stand.

Little Brother: Look, sis, I've got a deck of cards.
Big Sister: Big deal!

Miss Simons agreed to be interviewed by Alec for the school magazine.
"How old are you, Miss?" asked Alec.
"I'm not going to tell you that."
"But Mr Hill the technical teacher and Mr Hill the geography teacher told me how old they were."
"Oh well," said Miss Simon. "I'm the same age as both of them."
The poor teacher was not happy when she saw what Alec wrote: "Miss Simons, our English teacher, confided in me that she was as old as the Hills."

Why did the stupid boy wear a turtleneck sweater?
To hide his flea collar.

"Doctor, doctor, how can I avoid falling hair?"
"Step to one side."

Knock knock.
Who's there?
Passion.
Passion who?
Just Passion by and thought I'd pop
  in.

Knock knock.
Who's there?
Pickle.
Pickle who?
That's my favorite instrument.

Knock knock.
Who's there?
Phone.
Phone who?
Phone I'd known it was you.

Knock knock.
Who's there?
Pierre.
Pierre who?
Pierre through the keyhole – you'll
  see.

Knock knock.
Who's there?
Phyllis.
Phyllis who?
Phyllis up.

Did you hear about the boy who got worried when his nose grew to 11 inches long?
He thought it might turn into a foot.

"Doctor, doctor, this banana diet isn't working!"
"Stop scratching and come down from the curtains."

☆   ☆   ☆

"Doctor Sawbones speaking."
"Oh, doctor, my wife's just dislocated her jaw. Can you come over in, say, three or four weeks' time?"

☆   ☆   ☆

"I like your Easter tie."
"Why do you call it my Easter tie?"
"It's got egg on it."

☆   ☆   ☆

Why did the teacher have her hair in a bun?
Because she had her nose in a hamburger.

☆   ☆   ☆

How can you tell an old person from a young person?
An old person can sing and brush their teeth at the same time.

First Woman: Whenever I'm down in the dumps I buy myself a new hat.
Second Woman: Oh, so that's where you get them.

Britain's oldest lady was 115 years old today, and she hasn't got a gray hair on her head.
She's completely bald.

Fred: I was sorry to hear that your mother-in-law had died. What was the complaint?
Ted: We haven't had any yet.

My grandpa has so many wrinkles he has to screw his hat on.

☆ ☆ ☆

Uncle Hubert noticed that his nephew Johnny was watching him the whole time. "Why are you always looking at me?" he asked.
"I was just wondering when you were going to do your trick," replied Johnny.
"What trick?" inquired Uncle Hubert.
"Well, Mom and Dad say you drink like a fish."

My sister is so dumb, she thinks that a buttress is a female goat.

Knock knock.
Who's there?
Pill.
Pill who?
Pill you open the door?

Knock knock.
Who's there?
Pizza.
Pizza who?
Pizza this, piece of that.

Knock knock.
Who's there?
Pizza.
Pizza who?
Pizza the action.

Knock knock.
Who's there?
Plato.
Plato who?
Plato bacon and eggs, please.

Knock knock.
Who's there?
Plums.
Plums who?
Plums me you won't tell.

"I'd like a cheap parrot, please," an old lady said to a pet store owner.
"This one's cheap and it sings 'God Save The Queen.'"
"Never mind that," said the customer. "Is it tender?"

Would you say that a cannibal who ate his mother's sister was an aunt eater?

My auntie Mabel has got so many double chins it looks like she is peering over a pile of crumpets.

"Doctor, doctor, my left leg is giving me a lot of pain."
"I expect that's old age."
"But my right leg is as old, and that doesn't hurt at all!"

Doctor, doctor, I've just swallowed the film from my camera.
Well, let's hope nothing develops.

Did you hear about the granny who plugged her electric blanket into the toaster by mistake?
She spent the night popping out of bed.

Sandra's mother said no young man in his right mind would take her to the school dance in her bikini, so she decided to go with her friend's stupid brother.

I wouldn't say our English teacher is fat, but when she got on a Speak-Your-Weight machine it surrendered.

I never forget a face, but in your case I'll make an exception.

"Here's your Christmas present. A box of your favorite chocolates."
"Coo, thanks! But they're half empty!"
"Well, they're my favorites too!"

I can't get over that new beard of yours. It makes your face look just like a busted sofa.

What happened to the tailor who made his pants from sun-blind material?
Every time the sun came out, the pants rolled down.

Knock knock.
Who's there?
Pudding.
Pudding who?
Pudding our best feet forward.

Knock knock.
Who's there?
Pulp.
Pulp who?
Pulp pretty hard on the door – it's
   stiff.

Knock knock.
Who's there?
Punch.
Punch who?
Punch you on the nose if you don't
   shut up!

Knock knock.
Who's there?
Puss.
Puss who?
Puss the door – it won't open.

Knock knock.
Who's there?
Python.
Python who?
Python with your pocket money.

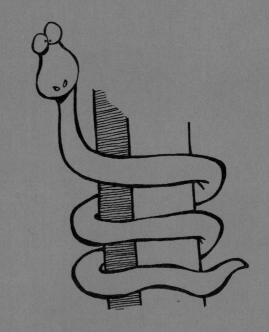

What is a dimple?
A pimple going the wrong way.

Girl: Shall I put the kettle on?
Boy: No, I think you look all right in the dress you're wearing.

Albert Littleun is so small his chin has a rash from his bootlaces.

Don't look out of the window, Lavinia, people will think it's Halloween.

First Middle-Aged Lady: I've kept my schoolgirl complexion.
Second Middle-Aged Lady: Yes, covered in spots.

My Auntie Edna is so fat, Uncle Tom has to stand up in bed each morning to see if it's daylight.

"What do you think of this photograph of me?"
"It makes you look older, frankly."
"Oh well, it'll save the cost of having another one taken later on."

Pompous Lady in Art Gallery: And I suppose that hideous-looking thing is a modern work of art?
Her Companion: Actually, it's a mirror.

What relation is a doorstep to a doormat?
Step-farther.

Did you hear about the time Eddy's sister tried to make a birthday cake? The candles melted in the oven.

Dotty Aunt Muriel received a letter one morning, and upon reading it burst into floods of tears. "What's the matter?" asked her companion. "Oh dear," sobbed Auntie. "It's my favorite nephew. He's got three feet." "Three feet?" exclaimed her friend. "Surely that's not possible?" "Well," said Auntie, "his mother's just written to tell me he's grown another foot!"

My uncle spent a fortune on deodorants before he found out that people didn't like him anyway.

Knock knock.
Who's there?
Raoul.
Raoul who?
Raoul of law.

Knock knock.
Who's there?
Rattlesnake.
Rattlesnake who?
Rattlesnake a big difference!

Knock knock.
Who's there?
Radio.
Radio who?
Radio not, it's time for school.

Knock knock.
Who's there?
Ray.
Ray who?
Ray drops keep falling on my head.

Knock knock.
Who's there?
Ralph.
Ralph who?
Ralph, ralph – I'm just a puppy.

Fatty: You look as if you've survived a famine – but only just.
Thinny: And you look as if you've caused one.

What is small, pink, wrinkly, and belongs to Grandpa?
Grandma.

Clarrie: Our math teacher has long black hair all down her back.
Barry: Yes, it's a pity it doesn't grow on her head.

"My uncle's got a wooden leg."
"That's nothing. My auntie has a wooden chest."

Mom! There's a man at the door collecting for the Old Folks' Home. Shall I give him Grandma?

Nell: What's the difference between your face and a sunset?
Ned: I don't know.
Nell: A sunset's beautiful.

"How old is your grandfather?"
"I dunno, but we've had him a long time."

"Mr Butcher, have you got a sheep's head?"
"No, madam, it's just the way I part my hair."

Simon: I was going to buy you a handkerchief for your birthday.
Sarah: That was a kind thought. But why didn't you?
Simon: I couldn't find one big enough for your nose.

Is that your face or are you wearing your hair back to front today?

"You youngsters are soft and lazy today. When I was your age I got up at six o'clock every morning and walked five or six miles before breakfast. I used to think nothing of it."
"I don't blame you, Grandpa. I wouldn't think much of it myself."

Boy: Have you heard of the idiot who keeps saying no?
Dad: No.

Knock knock.
Who's there?
Roach.
Roach who?
Roach out and touch somebody.

Knock knock.
Who's there?
Rio.
Rio who?
Riorrange your appointment please.

Knock knock.
Who's there?
Robert.
Robert who?
Roberts are taking over the world.

Knock knock.
Who's there?
Rita.
Rita who?
Rita novel.

Knock knock.
Who's there?
Robin.
Robin who?
Robin banks.

Susannah was watching her big sister covering her face with cream.
"What's that for?" she asked.
"To make me beautiful," came the reply. Susannah then watched in silence as her sister wiped her face clean.
"Doesn't work, does it?" she said.

"What's the secret of living to be 100?" the reporter asked the old man.
"Slugs!" replied the centenarian.
"Slugs?"
"Yes! I've never eaten one in my entire life!"

Chris: Do you like my new hairstyle?
Fliss: In as much as it covers most of your face, yes.

A very fat lady got on a crowded bus.
"Is no one going to give me a seat?" she boomed.
A very small man stood up and said, "I'll make a small contribution."

What did the idiot do to the flea in his ear?
Shot it!

Why did the idiot burn his ear?
He was listening to the match.

A small, thin, weedy little man went into a pub for a drink. He was fascinated by the barmaid, who was going bald, had droopy, bloodshot eyes, and was altogether extremely ugly. He turned to the man next to him and said, "What an amazing-looking woman!"
The man got hold of his coat collar and snarled, "That's my sister."
"Goodness," said the weedy little man. "Doesn't her face suit her!"

The number 93 bus was stuck in the rush hour traffic, when a very large lady turned to the man sitting next to her and said in a loud voice, "If you were a gentleman, you'd stand up and let one of those women sit down."
"And if you were a lady," replied the man, "you'd stand up and let all four of them sit down."

He's so thick that after he'd watched a gardening program on TV, he started watering the light bulbs.

Knock knock.
Who's there?
Rose.
Rose who?
Rose early one morning.

Knock knock.
Who's there?
Rosie.
Rosie who?
Rosie-lee is the best cuppa in the
    morning.

Knock knock.
Who's there?
Rosina.
Rosina who?
Rosina vase.

Knock knock.
Who's there?
Rothschild.
Rothschild who?
Rothschild is very clever.

Knock knock.
Who's there?
Roxie.
Roxie who?
Roxie Horror Show.

Knock knock.
Who's there?
Royal.
Royal who?
Royal show you his paintings if you
    ask nicely.

Jim: My sister wants to be an actress.
Tim: Is she pretty?
Jim: Well, put it this way, she'd be perfect on radio.

"You're ugly!"
"And you're drunk!"
"Yes, but in the morning I'll be sober!"

Doctor: Now tell me, Granny Perkins, how did you happened to burn both your ears.
Granny Perkins: I was doing the ironing when the telephone rang, and I picked up the iron and put that to my ear by mistake.
Doctor: But you burned both your ears!
Granny Perkins: Yes, well as soon as I put the phone down it rang again!

Did you hear about the boy who was known as Fog?
He was thick and wet.

What do sailors say when they see a fat person on a ship?
"A vast behind!"

A rather stern aunt had been staying with Sharon's parents, and one day she said to the little girl, "Well, Sharon, I'm going tomorrow. Are you sorry?"
"Oh yes, Auntie," replied Sharon. "I thought you were going today."

Peggy: I've just come back from the beauty parlor.
Piggy: Pity it was closed!

Maeve: You remind me of my favorite boxer.
Dave: Lennox Lewis?
Maeve: No, he's called Fido.

Patient: What does the X-ray of my brain show?
Doctor: Nothing.

"Are you writing a thank-you letter to Grandpa like I told you to?"
"Yes, Mom."
"Your handwriting seems very large."
"Well, Grandpa's very deaf, so I'm writing very loud."

Alfie had been listening to his sister practice her singing.
"Sis," he said, "I wish you'd sing Christmas carols."
"That's nice of you Alfie," she said. "Why?"
"Then I'd only have to hear you once a year!"

Knock knock.
Who's there?
Sacha.
Sacha who?
Sacha money in the bank.

Knock knock.
Who's there?
Sacha.
Sacha who?
Sacha lot of questions in this exam.

Knock knock.
Who's there?
Saddam.
Saddam who?
Saddam I that you couldn't come to
    the party.

Knock knock.
Who's there?
Saffron.
Saffron who?
Saffron a chair and it collapsed.

Knock knock.
Who's there?
Sally.
Sally who?
Sallyeverything you've got.

Knock knock.
Who's there?
Sam.
Sam who?
Sam day you'll recognize my voice.

I wouldn't say he's thick-headed – but he's the only person I know who's allowed to ride a motorbike without a helmet.

"I don't think these photographs you've taken do me justice."
"You don't want justice – you want mercy!"

☆　☆　☆

Mrs Saggy: Mrs Wrinkly tried to have a facelift last week.
Mrs Baggy: Tried to?
Mrs Saggy: Yes, they couldn't find a crane strong enough to lift her face!

☆　☆　☆

Molly: You've got a face like a million dollars.
Polly: What do you mean?
Molly: It's all green and wrinkled.

☆　☆　☆

Why did the middle-aged lady have to stop eating cream buns?
She was thick to her stomach.

☆　☆　☆

Marie: Two heads are better than one.
Gary: In your case none might be better than one!

Did you hear someone has invented a coffin that just covers the head? It's for people like you who are dead from the neck up!

Annie: People keep telling me I'm beautiful.
Andy: Some people have vivid imaginations.

☆ ☆ ☆

I wouldn't say Bertie has big ears but from the back he looks like the Soccer World Cup.

Son: But, Mom, they say I look like a werewolf.
Mom: Shut up and comb your face.

John: Do you feel like a cup of tea?
Don: Oh, yes.
John: You look like one, too – sloppy, hot and wet!

Roy: They say ignorance is bliss.
Rita: Then you should be the happiest boy in the world.

Knock knock.
Who's there?
Scott.
Scott who?
Scott land the brave.

☆　☆　☆

Knock knock.
Who's there?
Scott.
Scott who?
Scott nothing to do with you.

☆　☆　☆

Knock knock.
Who's there?
Scissor.
Scissor who?
Scissor was a Roman emperor.

☆　☆　☆

Knock knock.
Who's there?
Safari.
Safari who?
Safari, so good.

☆　☆　☆

Knock knock.
Who's there?
Scold.
Scold who?
Scold outside. Please let me in.

☆　☆　☆

"My brother said he'd tell me everything he knows."
"He must have been speechless."

The rain makes everything beautiful.
The grass and flowers too.
If the rain makes everything beautiful,
why doesn't it rain on you?

☆　　☆　　☆

Attendant in the Chamber of Horrors:
Could you keep moving on, please,
madam, we're stock-taking today.

☆　　☆　　☆

Gemma: I've been told I look just like an Italian dish.
Emma: You do.
Gemma: Really? Sophia Loren? Gina Lollobrigida?
Emma: No, spaghetti bolognese.

☆　　☆　　☆

Lyn: I don't like soup.
Bryn: I expect you can't get it to stay on the fork.

☆　　☆　　☆

Mrs Tiddles: Do you like my dress? I bought it for a very low price.
Mrs Toddles: You mean for a ridiculous figure.

"Does she have something on her mind?"
"Only if she's got a hat on."

Gill: Your sister uses too much make-up.
Jen: Do you think so?
Gill: Yes. It's so thick that if you tell her a joke, five minutes after she's stopped laughing her face is still smiling!

☆   ☆   ☆

My mother-in-law's so ugly she can make her own yogurt by staring at a pint of milk for an hour.

☆   ☆   ☆

Patient: The trouble is, doctor, I keep pulling ugly faces.
Doctor: Don't worry, I don't expect anyone will notice.

☆   ☆   ☆

Knock, knock.
Who's there?
Alec.
Alec who?
Alec most people but I don't like your face.

☆   ☆   ☆

Knock, knock.
Who's there?
Fred.
Fred who?
Fred I can't stand the sight of yours!

☆   ☆   ☆

Teddie: What's that terribly ugly thing on your shoulders?
Neddie: Help! What is it?
Teddie: Your head!

☆   ☆   ☆

Knock knock.
Who's there?
Seymour.
Seymour who?
Seymour from the top window.

Knock knock.
Who's there?
Sharon.
Sharon who?
Sharon share alike.

Knock knock.
Who's there?
Sheik and Geisha.
Sheik and Geisha who?
Sheik and Geisha'll find.

Knock knock.
Who's there?
Shelby.
Shelby who?
(sing) "Shelby coming round the
    mountain when she comes."

Knock knock.
Who's there?
Sherlock.
Sherlock who?
Sherlock your door – someone could
    break in.

Knock knock.
Who's there?
Sherry.
Sherry who?
Sherry trifle!

Sid: Mom, all the boys at school call me Big Head.

Mom: Never mind, love, just pop down to the shop for me and collect the ten pounds of potatoes I ordered in your cap.

Romeo: Your cheeks are like petals.

Juliet: Really?

Romeo: Yes, bicycle pedals.

I feel sorry for your little mind – all alone in that great big head.

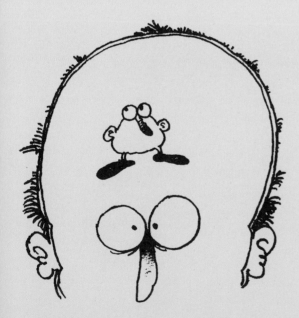

Jonathan ought to be a boxer. Someone might knock him conscious.

Jonah: Did you hear about Jim Jenkins's wife?

Mona: No, what about her?

Jonah: She's so ugly that when they got married, everyone kissed him.

John: How do you keep a thicko in suspense?

Jim: I don't know.

John: Tell you next week.

"When you're with him you need a long neck."
"Why?"
"Because your nose is then further away from his feet!"

Why did the idiot plant coins in his garden?
He wanted to raise some hard cash.

Jen: You look as if you'd find it hard to chew gum and walk at the same time.
Ken: And you look as if you'd find it hard to chew gum and breathe at the same time!

Neil: What's the difference between Nellie and a boring TV program?
Noel: You can turn off a boring TV program!

Jane: Do you ever do any gardening?
Wayne: Not often. Why?
Jane: You look as if you could do with some remedial weeding.

☆   ☆   ☆

Dylan: I take lots of exercise.
Duncan: I thought so. That's why you're so long-winded.

Knock knock.
Who's there?
Sigrid.
Sigrid who?
Sigrid Service.

Knock knock.
Who's there?
Simon.
Simon who?
Simon time again I've told you not to
    do that.

Knock knock.
Who's there?
Sis.
Sis who?
Sisteen Chapel.

Knock knock.
Who's there?
Sloane.
Sloane who?
Sloanely outside – let me in.

Knock knock.
Who's there?
Smarties.
Smarties who?
Smartiest kid in the class.

Knock knock.
Who's there?
Smee.
Smee who?
Smee, your friend.

Trixie: When I die I'm going to leave my brain to science.
Tracey: I suppose every little helps.

Brian: How long can someone live without a brain?
Ryan: How old are you?

Mick: Tim's gone to live in the city.
Nick: Why's that?
Mick: He'd read in the papers that the country was at war.

Man in Clothes Store: I'd like a blue shirt to match my eyes, please.
Sales Clerk: I'm sorry, sir, we don't have any blue shirts. But we do have some soft hats that would match your head.

What did the cookies say to the almonds?
"You're nuts and we're crackers!"

I always like to think the best of people, that's why I think of you as a complete idiot.

Madge: Your body's quite well organized.
Martin: How do you mean?
Madge: The weakest part – your brain – is protected by the strongest – your thick skull!

☆　☆　☆

Holly: Do you ever find life boring?
Dolly: I didn't until I met you.

☆　☆　☆

Lee: Our family's descended from royalty.
Dee: King Kong?

She's so stupid she thinks Christmas Eve is a tug of war.

Barry: You're like uncultivated woodland.
Gary: Really?
Barry: Yes, totally dense.

☆　☆　☆

He's so stupid he thinks a cucumber is something you play snooker with.

☆　☆　☆

Knock knock.
Who's there?
Snake.
Snake who?
Snake a run for it.

Knock knock.
Who's there?
Snickers.
Snickers who?
Snickers at me because I'm small.

Knock knock.
Who's there?
Snow.
Snow who?
Snow business of yours.

Knock knock.
Who's there?
Sondheim.
Sondheim who?
Sondheim soon we'll meet again.

Knock knock.
Who's there?
Sonia.
Sonia who?
Sonia shoe – it's stinking the house out!

Mary: Do you think my sister's pretty?
Gary: Well, let's just say if you pulled her pigtail she'd probably say "oink, oink"!

Avril: Sometimes I really like you.
April: When's that?
Avril: When you're not yourself.

Fat Lady: What's the best way to lose weight?
Thin Lady: Don't exceed the feed limit.

Ivan: They say Ian has a dual personality.
Ivor: Let's hope the other one is brighter than this one!

Handsome Harry: Every time I walk past a girl she sighs.
Wisecracking William: With relief!

Cheryl: They say I have an infectious laugh.
Meryl: In that case don't laugh near me!

"I hear she was a war baby."
"I'm not surprised – I expect her parents took one look at her and started fighting."

Cary: There's no point in telling you a joke with a double meaning.
Mary: Why not?
Cary: You wouldn't get either of them.

☆ ☆ ☆

Reg: I keep talking to myself.
Roger: I'm not surprised – no one else would listen to you!

☆ ☆ ☆

Nellie: I have an open mind.
Kelly: Yes, there's nothing in it.

☆ ☆ ☆

Zoe: I'm sure I'm right.
Chloe: You're as right as rain – all wet!

☆ ☆ ☆

Joey: What does "opaque" mean?
Josie: Something light can't pass through – like your head!

☆ ☆ ☆

She once had a million-dollar figure. Trouble is, inflation set in.

Knock knock.
Who's there?
Sonia.
Sonia who?
Sonia me!

Knock knock.
Who's there?
Sonny.
Sonny who?
Sonny outside, isn't it?

Knock knock.
Who's there?
Sophia.
Sophia who?
Sophia nothing . . . fear is pointless.

Knock knock.
Who's there?
Sorrel.
Sorrel who?
Sorrel about the mess.

Knock knock.
Who's there?
Soup.
Soup who?
Souper Mom!

Knock knock.
Who's there?
Spain.
Spain who?
Spaint all over the wall!

"I hear he has a quick mind."
"Yes, he's a real scheme engine."

Hazel: I wonder what my IQ is?
Heather: Don't worry about it, it's nothing.

☆ ☆ ☆

"He's got a chip on his shoulder."
"It's probably from the block of wood above."

☆ ☆ ☆

"She has great depth, you know."
"Yes, depth of ignorance."

☆ ☆ ☆

"She has a mind of her own."
"Of course she does. No one else would want it."

☆ ☆ ☆

Bennie: I've been told I must lose 10 pounds of surplus fat.
Kenny: You could always cut off your head.

☆ ☆ ☆

Bill: I never act stupid.
Hil: No, with you it's the real thing.

"You can read his mind in his face."
"Yes, it's usually a complete blank."

☆　☆　☆

Jane: I'll cook dinner. What would you like?
Shane: Good life insurance.

First Explorer: There's one thing about Jenkinson.
Second Explorer: What's that?
First Explorer: He could go to headhunters' country without any fear – they'd have no interest in him.

☆　☆　☆

"I've been thinking hard about what you said."
"You mean it's hard for you to think."

☆　☆　☆

Stella: Tracey has a ready wit.
Sheila: Perhaps she could let us know when it's ready!

☆　☆　☆

Daniel: Being clever isn't everything.
Denzil: In your case it isn't anything.

☆　☆　☆

"They call him Baby-Face."
"Does that mean he has a brain to match?"

☆　☆　☆

In one way Julian is lucky. If he went out of his mind, no one would notice the difference.

☆　☆　☆

Knock knock.
Who's there?
Stalin.
Stalin who?
Stalin for time.

Knock knock.
Who's there?
Stan.
Stan who?
Stan back, I'm going to be sick.

Knock knock.
Who's there?
Stan and Della.
Stan and Della who?
Stan and Dellaver.

Knock knock.
Who's there?
Stefan.
Stefan who?
Stefan it!

Knock knock.
Who's there?
Stella.
Stella who?
Stella lot from the rich people.

Harry's very good for other people's health.
Whenever they see him coming they go for a long walk!

"Why is your brother always flying off the handle?"
"Because he's got a screw loose."

☆　☆　☆

"His speech started at 2 p.m. sharp."
"And finished at 3 p.m. dull."

☆　☆　☆

They say many doctors have examined her brain – but they can't find anything in it.

☆　☆　☆

Laura: Whenever I go to the local store the storekeeper shakes my hand.
Lionel: I expect it's to make sure you don't put it in his till.

☆　☆　☆

Don't let your mind wander. It's not strong enough to be allowed out on its own.

Jerry: Is that a new perfume I smell?
Kerry: It is, and you do!

"I'd say he was spineless."
"Yes, about as spineless as cooked spaghetti."

Son: How old are you, Dad?
Dad: Oh, around 35.
Son: I expect you've been around it a few times!

"Did you say he had a big mouth?"
"Put it this way, he's the only person I know who can eat a banana sideways!"

Fenton: You'll just have to give me credit.
Benton: Well, I'm certainly not giving you cash!

"He reminds me of a bowl of custard."
"Yes, yellow and thick."

Knock knock.
Who's there?
Stephanie.
Stephanie who?
Stephanie gas – we need to go
    faster!

Knock knock.
Who's there?
Steve.
Steve who?
Steve upper lip.

Knock knock.
Who's there?
Stevie.
Stevie who?
Stevie has terrible reception.

Knock knock.
Who's there?
Stones.
Stones who?
Stones sober.

☆   ☆   ☆

Knock knock.
Who's there?
Stopwatch.
Stopwatch who?
Stopwatch you're doing this minute!

☆   ☆   ☆

Knock knock.
Who's there?
Street.
Street who?
Street to go out to dinner.

☆   ☆   ☆

When my dad finally passed his exam for junior high school he was so excited he cut himself shaving.

Mother: Anne, why are you making faces at the bulldog?
Anne: Well, he started it.

Jimmy: Is that lemonade OK?
Timmy: Yes. Why do you ask?
Jimmy: I just wondered if it was as sour as your face.

☆   ☆   ☆

Anne: Do you think I look awful in this dress?
Dan: You could look worse – if I had better eyesight!

He thinks everyone worships the ground he crawled out of.

☆   ☆   ☆

Jan: My little brother is a real pain.
Nan: Things could be worse.
Jan: How?
Nan: He could be twins.

"He has a heart of gold."
"And teeth to match."

☆   ☆   ☆

"He's a light eater."
"Yes, as soon as it's light he starts eating!"

Will: Why do you call that new player Cinderella?
Bill: Because he's always running away from the ball.

"My sister went on a crash diet."
"Is that why she looks a wreck?"

☆ ☆ ☆

"My brother's on a seafood diet."
"Really?"
"Yes, the more he sees food, the more he eats."

☆ ☆ ☆

"My mother gets migraine."
"Probably because her halo's too tight."

☆ ☆ ☆

Winnie: I was cut out to be a genius.
Ginnie: Pity no one put the pieces together properly.

☆ ☆ ☆

"How can she be so fat? She eats like a bird!"
"Yes, a vulture!"

☆ ☆ ☆

"Does he have a big mouth?"
"Put it this way, he can sing a duet by himself."

☆ ☆ ☆

Jake: That ointment the veterinarian gave me for the dog makes my fingers smart.
Blake: Why don't you rub some on your head then?

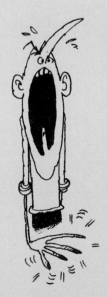

Knock knock.
Who's there?
Tamsin.
Tamsin who?
Tamsin time again I come to the
   wrong house.

Knock knock.
Who's there?
Tango.
Tango who?
Tango faster than this you know.

Knock knock.
Who's there?
Talbot.
Talbot who?
Talbot too thin.

Knock knock.
Who's there?
Tania.
Tania who?
Tania self round, you'll see.

Knock knock.
Who's there?
Tamara.
Tamara who?
Tamara's the day of the school
   concert.

Terry: When my mother was young she had a coming-out party.

Gerry: When they saw her they probably sent her back in again.

"Do you like my new baby sister? The stork brought her."

"Hmm, it looks as if the stork dropped her on her head."

"His left eye must be fascinating."

"Why do you say that?"

"Because his right eye looks at it all the time."

"Did the medicine I gave your Uncle straighten him out?"

"It sure did. They buried him today."

A tramp knocked on the door and asked the lady of the house for some food. "Didn't I give you a slice of gooseberry tart a week ago?" she asked.

"Yes," said the tramp, "but I'm a lot better now."

"That girl looks like Helen Black."
"She looks even worse in white."

"Bill and Gill make a perfect pair, don't they?"
"They certainly do. She's a pill and he's a headache."

Lady: (to a tramp begging for a meal) Do you like cold prunes and custard?
Tramp: I love it lady.
Lady: Well, call back later, it is very hot right now.

She's so ugly that when a wasp stings her it shuts its eyes.

"He will never be a leader of men."
"No, but he's a great follower of women!"

"Doesn't he look distinguished?"
"He'd look better if he were extinguished."

"They say she has a sharp tongue."
"Yes, she can slice bread with it."

Knock knock.
Who's there?
Tara.
Tara who?
Tararaboomdeay.

Knock knock.
Who's there?
Tariq.
Tariq who?
Tariq of perfume will put anyone off.

Knock knock.
Who's there?
Tarzan.
Tarzan who?
Tarzan stripes forever!

Knock knock.
Who's there?
Teacher.
Teacher who?
Teacher-self French.

Knock knock.
Who's there?
Teacher.
Teacher who?
Teacher to copy my answers!

"They say cleanliness is next to godliness."
"With some people it's next to impossible!"

"Does he tell lies?"
"Let's just say his memory exaggerates."

"They say he's going places."
"The sooner the better!"

What happened when the monster had a brain transplant? The brain rejected him.

From a newspaper: Because the elderly find it difficult to climb the hill, the council has agreed to put a seat at the top.

Maureen: I hear Mattie likes field hockey.
Doreen: That's because she's such a bully!

"I always think twice before speaking."
"I expect it gives you time to think up something really nasty."

First Neighbor: How old do you think I am?

Second Neighbor: I don't know, but I've heard your grandfather was called Adam.

"Did you say he told good gags?"
"No, I said he needed one!"

☆　☆　☆

When it comes to helping others, she'll stop at nothing!

☆　☆　☆

"She has real polish."
"Only on her shoes."

☆　☆　☆

"She always has an answer to every problem."
"Yes, but they're always wrong."

☆　☆　☆

Dickie: I hear the team's prospects are looking up.
Nicky: Oh good, are you leaving it then?

☆　☆　☆

Why did the violinist stand on the roof?
So he could reach the high notes.

Knock knock.
Who's there?
Teheran.
Teheran who?
Teheran and look me in the eye.

Knock knock.
Who's there?
Teheran.
Teheran who?
Teheran very slowly – there's a
    monster behind you.

Knock knock.
Who's there?
Telly.
Telly who?
Telly your friend to come out.

Knock knock.
Who's there?
Tennis.
Tennis who?
Tennis five plus five.

Knock knock.
Who's there?
Tennis.
Tennis who?
Tennis two times five.

Novice Tennis Player: How would you have played that last shot?
Coach: In disguise!

She could give a headache to an aspirin!

☆　　☆　　☆

"He's watching his weight."
"Yes, watching it go up!"

☆　　☆　　☆

"Does he have big ears?"
"Let's just say he's very good at swatting flies."

☆　　☆　　☆

She's got so fat she can sit around a table all by herself.

☆　　☆　　☆

"Your teeth are like the stars," he said,
as he pressed her hand, so white.
He spoke the truth, for, like the stars, her teeth came out at night!

☆　　☆　　☆

"He thinks he's a big cheese."
"I certainly have to hold my nose when I'm near him."

What do you call a gorilla with a banana in each ear?
Anything you like, because he can't hear you.

☆ ☆ ☆

Man: Can I have a canary for my wife please?
Pet Store Owner: I'm sorry, sir, we don't do swaps.

☆ ☆ ☆

The last time I saw a face like yours I threw it a banana.

He's the kind of boy girls dream about.
That's better than seeing him in broad daylight.

Man in Café: I don't like this gooseberry pie.
Woman Cook: Well, I'll have you know I was making gooseberry pie before you were born.
Man: Perhaps this is one of them.

☆ ☆ ☆

Customer: Two soggy eggs on burned toast, please.
Café Owner: We can't serve that here, sir.
Customer: Why not, you did yesterday.

☆ ☆ ☆

Knock knock.
Who's there?
Termite.
Termite who?
Termite's the night!

Knock knock.
Who's there?
Thatcher.
Thatcher who?
Thatcher car? Rubbish, innit!

Knock knock.
Who's there?
Thea.
Thea who?
Thea later alligator.

Knock knock.
Who's there?
Thea.
Thea who?
Thea ghost?

Knock knock.
Who's there?
Theodore.
Theodore who?
Theodore is locked.

The problem is, his facial features don't seem to understand the importance of being part of a team.

What did the fat man say when someone suggested he should take up golf?
"It's no use – if I put the ball where I can see it I can't hit it, and if I put it where I can hit it I can't see it."

Terry: I spend hours in front of the mirror admiring my looks. Do you think that's vanity?
Jerry: No, just a vivid imagination.

What did they call the crazy golfer?
A crack putt!

Why didn't the idiot go water-skiing when he was on vacation?
He couldn't find a sloping lake.

Beanpole Brenda was so thin she could:
Hide behind a bus stop.
Disappear when she stood sideways.
Have difficulty preventing herself from slipping down the drain when she took a bath.
Be mistaken for a mop when her hair needed cutting.
Hide up a tree, even in winter.

She's so poisonous that if a snake bit her it would die.

Gorging Gordon was so large he could:
Take a shower without getting his feet wet.
Make a room dark by standing in front of the window.
Fill up the entire back seat of a car.
Have mumps without anyone realizing it.

For Sale: Antique porcelain vase, property of elderly lady only slightly cracked.

"She's a wonderful player. I'd say she was one in a million."
"Really? I thought she was won in a raffle."

Grandma: I have the face of a teenager.
Grandchild: Then you'd better give it back, you're getting it all wrinkled!

Gemma: I see more of John than I used to.
Emma: Yes, he's certainly put on weight recently.

Knock knock.
Who's there?
Thighs.
Thighs who?
Thighs the limit.

Knock knock.
Who's there?
Thistle.
Thistle who?
Thistle be the last time I knock.

☆   ☆   ☆

Knock knock.
Who's there?
Theresa.
Theresa who?
Theresa green.

Knock knock.
Who's there?
Thomas.
Thomas who?
Thomaster a language takes a long
    time.

☆   ☆   ☆

Knock knock.
Who's there?
Thermos.
Thermos who?
Thermos be a better player than
    you.

Did you hear about the two fat boys who ran in a race?
One ran in short bursts; the other in burst shorts.

Despondent Golfer: I'd move heaven and earth to get a better score.
Caddie: Concentrate on heaven, you've already moved enough earth!

Boss: It would take ten men to fill my shoes.
Secretary, aside: It looks as if it took ten cows to make them.

Harold: We should all try to fight air pollution.
Henry: You could start by stopping breathing.

Brian: Shall I put the telly on?
Ryan: It might look better than that shirt you're wearing.

"They say her chin was her best feature."
"It's now a double feature."

Your cheeks are like peaches –
football peetches.

Samantha: Don't I look gorgeous
today?
Susannah: It's a treat for people to
see you. After all, they have to pay to
get into a freak show.

"If I were a member of the Noise
Abatement Society I'd send her a
button."
"For her jacket?"
"No, for her lips."

Peter: Her cooking gives food for
thought.
Paul: It certainly doesn't give food for
eating!

☆   ☆   ☆

She's always talking with her mouth
full – of words!

☆   ☆   ☆

He's not really an upright character.
In fact, even his shadow is crooked.

Sister: How do you cook sausages in a
jungle?
Brother: Under a gorilla!

☆   ☆   ☆

He's so stupid he probably couldn't
spell "Anna" backwards.

Knock knock.
Who's there?
Throat.
Throat who?
Throat to me.

☆   ☆   ☆

Knock knock.
Who's there?
Thumb.
Thumb who?
Thumb like it hot.

Knock knock.
Who's there?
Thumping.
Thumping who?
Thumping green and slimy is
    creeping up your leg.

☆   ☆   ☆

Knock knock.
Who's there?
Thumping.
Thumping who?
Thumping's jutht knocked my teef
    out.

☆   ☆   ☆

Knock knock.
Who's there?
Tic tac.
Tic tac who?
Tic tac paddy whack, give the dog a
    bone.

☆   ☆   ☆

"She's a great girl.
Everybody loves her!"
"Yes, thousands of
fleas can't all be
wrong!"

His clothes never go out of style –
they look just as old-fashioned every
year.

"I'm as pretty as a flower."
"Yes, a cauliflower."

☆   ☆   ☆

"He can't see further than the nose
on his face."
"No, but with his nose that's quite a
distance."

Norman: Nigel plays the mouth
organ. He's had many requests.
Norma: So I've heard. But he keeps
on playing anyway.

"You know how nurses slap babies
when they are born?"
"Yes."
"Well, when you were born I reckon
they took one look and slapped your
mother."

Tara: I've got a mechanical mind.
Tommy: Yes, but some of
your screws are loose.

He's so bald you can't look at him in bright sunlight without wearing sunglasses.

"What do you think of Ada's looks?"
"I don't mind her looking, it's her face I can't stand."

"Why do you say he's got tennis-match eyes?"
"He's so cross-eyed he can watch both ends of the court without moving his head."

"They say when the photographer took Jim's photograph he never developed it."
"Why?"
"He was afraid of being alone with it in a dark room."

"Words fail me."
"I'd noticed you don't know how to use them."

George: I'm not waiting in this line, I'm going in front of you!
Graham: Good, it means I won't have to look at your face.

Knock knock.
Who's there?
Tick.
Tick who?
Tick 'em up and gimme all your
    money.

Knock knock.
Who's there?
Tiffany.
Tiffany who?
Tiffany rubbish out of the bag
    before you use it.

Knock knock.
Who's there?
Tilly.
Tilly who?
Tilly learns to say please, he'll stay
    outside.

Knock knock.
Who's there?
Tilly.
Tilly who?
Tilly cows come home.

Knock knock.
Who's there?
Tim.
Tim who?
Tim after time.

Knock knock.
Who's there?
Tim.
Tim who?
Tim you got scared.

"My girlfriend loves nature."
"That's very good of her, considering what nature has done to her!"

He's such a whinger, if opportunity knocked he'd complain about the noise.

"Do you think I have a good complexion?"
"Let's just say your face is almost as smooth as a walnut."

Rosie: I like being tickled under the chin.
Josie: Which one?

☆   ☆   ☆

"His teeth are all his own."
"Has he finally finished paying for them, then?"

Will: What's the difference between Robin Hood and you?
Bill: I don't know.
Will: Robin was a big hero; you're a big zero.

Jenny: Do you like my new suit? I'm told it fits like a glove.
Lenny: Yes, it sticks out in five places.

☆   ☆   ☆

"She's not very fat, is she?"
"No, she's got a really faminine look."
"Her sister's skinny, too."
"Yes, if she drinks tomato juice, she looks like a thermometer."

Millie: I've been told I'm out of this world.
Willy: Many people wish you were!

Mary: Everyone says I've got a big mouth. What should I do?
Gary: Buy a bigger toothbrush?

"She's a woman of many parts."
"Pity they were put together so badly."

Did you hear about the boy who sat under a cow?
He got a pat on the head.

He's so cold-blooded that if a mosquito bit him, it would get pneumonia.

Knock knock.
Who's there?
Tina.
Tina who?
Tina tomatoes.

Knock knock.
Who's there?
Toby.
Toby who?
Toby or not Toby, that is the
     question.

Knock knock.
Who's there?
Toffee.
Toffee who?
Toffeel loved is the best feeling in
     the world.

Knock knock.
Who's there?
Tommy.
Tommy who?
Tommy you will always be beautiful.

Knock knock.
Who's there?
Tom Sawyer.
Tom Sawyer who?
Tom Sawyer bum when you were
     changing your trousers.

"Do you know what we'd get if we crossed you with a bottom?"
"What?"
"A no-good bum."

Susie: I think a lot of people would go to our principal's funeral.
Sally: Yes, to make sure she's dead!

His death won't be listed under "Obituaries," it will be under "Neighborhood Improvements."

Jimmy: Go and squirt lemon juice in your eyes.
Timmy: Whatever for?
Jimmy: It's the only way to make you smart.

☆   ☆   ☆

Anne: Where are you in the class photo?
Dan, pointing: There.
Anne: Oh, I didn't recognize you. I've never seen you with your mouth shut before.

Claud: What's the difference between you and a skunk?
Maud: I don't know.
Claud: You use a cheaper deodorant.

Cary: Your face should be painted in oils.
Mary: Why, because I'm beautiful?
Cary: No, because you've got a face like a sardine.

Singer: Did you like my sad song?
Listener: Sad? I'd call it pitiful!

"There are a lot of fans at his concerts."
"I expect it's because the management can't run to air-conditioning."

He's such a puny weakling, if he ever gets married they won't throw confetti, they'll throw vitamin pills.

"They say he's a millionaire, and lives in a 20-room mansion, but he always looks grubby and doesn't smell too good."
"I guess he's just filthy rich."

Knock knock.
Who's there?
Too whit.
Too whit who?
Is there an owl in the house?

Knock knock.
Who's there?
Topic.
Topic who?
Topic a wild flower is against the
   law.

Knock knock.
Who's there?
Tori.
Tori who?
Tori I upset you.

Knock knock.
Who's there?
Toto.
Toto who?
Totolly devoted to you.

Knock knock.
Who's there?
Taipei.
Taipei who?
Taipei sixty words a minute is pretty
   fast!

...ter singing's like an old car – it needs a tune-up.

"You're like a summer cold!"
"What do you mean?"
"It's impossible to get rid of you!"

Harry: How do you spell "nutcase" with just one letter?
Larry: I don't know.
Harry: U.

Bobbie: You'd make a perfect . . .
Nobbie: What?
Bobbie: Stranger!

What's the difference between a bully and a clock?
One goes "tick, tock," the other's a thick tock.

"You're very ugly."
"Yes, and you're quite good-looking – for a gorilla, that is."

Julie: I don't know what to buy Granddad for Christmas. He's so rich – what do you buy a man who has everything?
Johnny: A watchdog?

"You remind me of a toenail."
"What do you mean?"
"The sooner you're cut down to size the better."

"You're like an oil well."
"What do you mean?"
"Always boring."

Darren: I'm so thirsty my tongue's hanging out.
Sharon: Is that your tongue? I thought it was a horrible spotted tie!

Sue: You'd make a good exchange student.
Pru: Do you think so?
Sue: Yes. We might be able to exchange you for someone nice.

James: Do you know what nice people do at the weekend?
John: No.
James: I didn't think you would.

Knock knock.
Who's there?
Toyota.
Toyota who?
Toyota be a law against people like you.

Knock knock.
Who's there?
Tracy.
Tracy who?
Tracy the shape in pencil.

Knock knock.
Who's there?
Tricia.
Tricia who?
Bless you – what a bad cold!

Knock knock.
Who's there?
Tristan.
Tristan who?
Tristan insect to really get up your nose.

Knock knock.
Who's there?
Tristan.
Tristan who?
Tristan elephant not to forget.

Knock knock.
Who's there?
Troy.
Troy who?
Troy the bell instead.

"Why do you call her 'Amazon'? Is it because she's big and strong?"
"No, just rather wide."

Kate: I always speak my mind.
Kath: I'm surprised you've so much to say, then.

What's the difference between a bully and gravy?
Gravy's only thick some of the time.

"He's a person of rare intelligence."
"Yes, he hasn't got much."

Denise: Your panty hose is all wrinkled.
Doreen: But I'm not wearing panty hose.

"You're like a remote control."
"How do you mean?"
"You turn everybody off."

"Let's just say he's got a hat full of cement."
"What do you mean?"
"He's a blockhead."

☆　　☆　　☆

Jean: Did you know we could get fur from you?
Dean: Really? What sort?
Jean: As fur as possible!

☆　　☆　　☆

352

Knock, knock.
Who's there?
Stan.
Stan who?
Stan back, his breath smells awful!

Heavy: This place isn't big enough for the two of us.
Harvey: You'd better go on a diet, then!

Stella: You only have one use in life.
Ella: What's that?
Stella: Your face can cure hiccups!

Barry: I reckon you weren't brought by a stork, Bob, you were brought by a vulture.

John: I'd hate to be in your shoes.
Con: And I'd hate to be in yours – I know what your feet smell like!

Glynn: You remind me of a builder's bottom.
Wynn: What do you mean?
Glynn: You're full of barefaced cheek!

Knock knock.
Who's there?
Trudy.
Trudy who?
Trudy your word.

Knock knock.
Who's there?
Truffle.
Truffle who?
Truffle with you is you are so shy.

Knock knock.
Who's there?
Truman.
Truman who?
Truman and good needed for the
    jury.

Knock knock.
Who's there?
Trump.
Trump who?
Trumped-up charges.

Knock knock.
Who's there?
Tubby.
Tubby who?
Tubby or not to be.

Knock knock.
Who's there?
Tummy.
Tummy who?
Tummy you'll always be the best.

"What do you mean she eats like a bird? She's enormous!"
"I expect she eats worms."

Why did the silly girl throw her guitar away?
Because it had a hole in it.

Mrs Feather: I'm off to get my hair done.
Mr Feather: Going to the ugly parlor again, are you?

Jerry: I feel like a strawberry.
Terry: You are in a jam, aren't you?

Mother: If you eat your greens you'll grow up to be a beautiful young woman.
Millie: Why didn't you eat your greens when you were young?

Jane: How often do you go to the dentist?
Wayne: Twice a year.
Jane: Once for each tooth?

Brenda: My dad says intelligence reigns supreme in our family.
Glenda: But it obviously didn't rain the day you were born.

Jean: Doctor, how can I avoid this run-down feeling?
Doctor: Try looking both ways before you cross the road.

Eustace: I feel like an onion.
Esmond: You are in a pickle.

Norbert: You remind me of a pie.
Noreen: Really? Am I sweet?
Norbert: No, but you've got some crust.

Ronnie: Why are you bathing in such dirty water?
Donnie: It wasn't dirty when I got in it.

Knock knock.
Who's there?
Tuna.
Tuna who?
Tuna whole orchestra.

Knock knock.
Who's there?
Turin.
Turin who?
Turin to a werewolf under a full
    moon.

Knock knock.
Who's there?
Turkey.
Turkey who?
Turkey then you can open the door.

Knock knock.
Who's there?
Turner.
Turner who?
Turner round, there's a monster
    breathing down your neck.

Knock knock.
Who's there?
Turnip.
Turnip who?
Turnip for work at nine or you're
    fired!

They're very well matched. She's blinded by love and his looks are out of sight.

Bernie: What's the matter with your finger?
Ernie: I think I have a splinter in it.
Bernie: Have you been scratching your head?

Angus: Have you been talking to yourself again?
Adam: Yes, how did you know?
Angus: You've got that bored look.

Mother: What did you do to make my little Susie cry, Simon?
Simon: I didn't do anything. In fact, I paid her a compliment.
Mother: What did you say?
Simon: I said she smelled less than any girl I'd ever known.

"She's got a figure like school custard."
"How do you mean?"
"Very lumpy!"

What lies at the bottom of the sea and shivers?
A nervous wreck.

☆　☆　☆

Patty: What smells worse than a bad egg?
Mattie: I don't know.
Patty: You do!

☆　☆　☆

You're like an orange – you give me the pip.

Visitor: You're very quiet, Jennifer.
Jennifer: Well, my Mum gave me a dollar not to say anything about your red nose.

Diner: This food isn't fit for a pig!
Waiter: I'll bring you some that is, sir.

☆　☆　☆

"How can I sharpen my appetite?"
"Try eating razor blades."

☆　☆　☆

Knock knock.
Who's there?
UB40.
UB40 who?
UB40 today – happy birthday!

Knock knock.
Who's there?
Uganda.
Uganda who?
Uganda go away now.

Knock knock.
Who's there?
Una.
Una who?
Yes, Una who.

Knock knock.
Who's there?
Underwear.
Underwear who?
Underwear my baby is tonight?

Knock knock.
Who's there?
Uttica.
Uttica who?
(sing) "Uttica high road and I'll take
           the low road."

Gilly: Do you like my cottage pie?
Billy: No, it tastes as if you've left the drains in it.

Dick: Why do you smell so peculiar?
Rick: It's soap – I might have known you wouldn't recognize the smell.

"Why do you say I remind you of a vampire?"
"You have bat breath."

Mo: Why do you think the Neverbath football team will win?
Joe: They smell so bad no one will ever dare tackle them!

"You're like the Mona Lisa."
"You mean I've got a beautiful smile?"
"No, your face is all dirty and cracked."

Did you hear about the witch who turned her friend into an egg?
She kept trying to poach her ideas.

"You're like an old king."
"What do you mean?"
"You should be throne away."

Lizzie: Listening to you is like hearing a dripping faucet.
Dizzy: How do you mean?
Lizzie: You can always hear it but you can't turn it off.

Susie: Do you think I'm looking good?
Simon: You've never looked better in your life – whenever that was.

Large Lady: Could you see me across the street, young man?
Cheeky Charlie: You're so large I could see you across the county!

Woman in Beauty Parlor: What would it take to make me look good?
Proprietor: A fair distance!

Romeo: You should have been born in the Dark Ages.
Juliet: Why?
Romeo: You look awful in the light.

Knock knock.
Who's there?
Vampire.
Vampire who?
Vampire State Building.

Knock knock.
Who's there?
Vanda.
Vanda who?
Vanda you vant me to come round?

Knock knock.
Who's there?
Vanessa.
Vanessa who?
Vanessa time I'll ring the bell.

Knock knock.
Who's there?
Vault.
Vault who?
Vaultsing Matilda.

Knock knock.
Who's there?
Venice.
Venice who?
Venice this going to end?

How can you keep a very sweaty man from smelling?
Cut off his nose!

Dave: Is your sister beautiful?
Don: Well, if she were a building I'd say she'd be condemned.

When he was a baby he was so ugly his parents ran away from home.

Mrs Mugface: How your little daughter's grown!
Mrs Jugface: Yes, she certainly gruesome.

Patient: My hair seems to be getting thinner.
Doctor: Why do you want fat hair?

"I've heard she's fat and ugly."
"I'll say. When she goes to the doctor, he tells her to open her mouth and say 'Moo.'"

Mrs Flabby: I've managed to keep my weight down this year.
Mrs Tabby: Yes, down in the same place.

Two actors were talking about a glamorous young starlet. "I like her dresses," said the first.

"Yes," replied the second. "They certainly seem to bring out the bust in her."

Gordon: I think I've got a sixth sense.
Jordan: You must have, because there's no sign of the other five.

Mickey: Why do you say I'm like blotting paper?
Dickey: You soak everything up but you get it all backwards.

Nellie: Is your auntie old?
Kelly: Old? When she was born Billy wasn't even a kid!

They say his violin playing is improving. People only put earplugs in one ear now.

His teeth stick out so much I thought his nose was playing a piano.

Footballer: I've a good idea to improve the team.
Manager: Good. When are you leaving?

Knock knock.
Who's there?
Verdi.
Verdi who?
Verdia want to go?

Knock knock.
Who's there?
Vic.
Vic who?
Victim of a vampire.

Knock knock.
Who's there?
Vic.
Vic who?
Victory parade.

Knock knock.
Who's there?
Victor.
Victor who?
Victor his football shorts.

Knock knock.
Who's there?
Vincent.
Vincent who?
Vincent alive anymore.

Knock knock.
Who's there?
Vincent.
Vincent who?
Vincent me here.

That singer only got to the top because her dresses didn't.

Andy: My dad's stronger than your dad.
Mandy: He must be after raising a dumb-bell like you!

An American tourist was visiting a quaint country village, and got talking to an old man in the local pub. "And have you lived here all your life, sir?" asked the American.
"Not yet, m'dear," said the villager wisely.

Louise: What's the difference between you and a baby lamb?
Lionel: I don't know.
Louise: The lamb will one day be a sheep, but you'll always be a creep.

Lesley: Did she really call you a creep?
Wesley: Yes. She said I was lower than the fluff in an earthworm's belly button.

"I think I'm a little overweight."
"Nonsense! Pull up three chairs and we'll talk about it."

Sandy: Do you like going to the movies?

Mandy: The trouble with most movies is that they shoot too much film and not enough actors.

Ronnie: I can trace my family tree way back.

Bonnie: Yes, back to the time you lived in it!

"What will you do when you're as big as your dad?"

"Go on a diet!"

"Dad, do slugs taste nice?"

"Of course not, why do you ask?"

"Because you've just eaten one that was in your salad."

Knock, knock.

Who's there?

Anatole.

Anatole who?

Anatole me you were hopeless.

Your beard looks as if it goes to the same veterinarian as my dog.

Knock knock.
Who's there?
Viola.
Viola who?
Viola sudden you don't know who I
    am?

Knock knock.
Who's there?
Violet.
Violet who?
Violet the cat out of the bag.

Knock knock.
Who's there?
Violin.
Violin who?
Violin horrible boy.

Knock knock.
Who's there?
Viper.
Viper who?
Viper your nose!

☆   ☆   ☆

Knock knock.
Who's there?
Visa.
Visa who?
Visa the ones you want.

☆   ☆   ☆

Knock knock.
Who's there?
Voodoo.
Voodoo who?
Voodoo you think you are?

☆   ☆   ☆

Knock knock.
Who's there?
Wade.
Wade who?
Wading room.

Knock knock.
Who's there?
Walter.
Walter who?
Walter, walter everywhere and not a
    drop to drink.

Knock knock.
Who's there?
Walter.
Walter who?
Walter wall carpet.

Knock knock.
Who's there?
Ward.
Ward who?
Ward you want?

Knock knock.
Who's there?
Watson.
Watson who?
Watson your head, it looks
    disgusting!

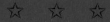

William: Bob's so suspicious, isn't he?
Wilfred: Yes. Even his eyes watch each other all the time.

Mother: Why is your little sister crying?
Jimmy: Because I won't give her my sandwich.
Mother: What about her own sandwich?
Jimmy: She cried when I ate that too.

What should you give short elves?
Elf-raising flour.

Did you hear about the witch who was so ugly she kept sending her mirror back for repairs?

"My auntie has a sore throat. What should she do?"
"Take aunti-septic."

Mr Smooth was ordering a meal in a restaurant and was horrified to see that the waiter was covered with pimples.
"Have you got acne?" he asked.
"No," replied the waiter, "just what you can see on the menu."

Knock knock.
Who's there?
Watson.
Watson who?
Watson the menu today?

Knock knock.
Who's there?
Wayne.
Wayne who?
(sing) "Wayne in a manger, no crib
    for a bed."

Knock knock.
Who's there?
Webster.
Webster who?
Webster Spin, your friendly
    neighborhood spider.

Knock knock.
Who's there?
Wedgewood.
Wedgewood who?
Wedgewood come if he could but
    he's busy.

☆   ☆   ☆

Knock knock.
Who's there?
Weevil.
Weevil who?
Weevil work it out.

☆   ☆   ☆

Knock knock.
Who's there?
Weevil.
Weevil who?
Weevil make you talk.

☆   ☆   ☆

Knock knock.
Who's there?
Wendy.
Wendy who?
Wendy come to take you away I
    won't stop them!

Knock knock.
Who's there?
Wendy.
Wendy who?
Wendy weather we're having.

Knock knock.
Who's there?
Wesley.
Wesley who?
Wesley wind is blowing out here.

Knock knock.
Who's there?
Whelk.
Whelk who?
Whelk-ome home.

Knock knock.
Who's there?
White.
White who?
White in the middle of it.

Knock knock.
Who's there?
Whitney.
Whitney who?
Whitneyssed the crime.

A man sat on a train chewing gum and staring vacantly into space, when suddenly an old woman sitting opposite said, "It's no good you talking to me, young man, I'm stone deaf!"

Two old friends met, ten years after the end of the Second World War. One said, "Is that your face or are you still wearing your gas mask?"

"You are so ugly your face would stop a clock."
"And yours would make one run."

Emma: I'd like to say something nice about you as it's your birthday.
Gemma: Why don't you?
Emma: Because I can't think of a single thing to say!

She's so stupid she thinks a shoplifter is a very strong person who goes round picking up shops.

(374)

Knock knock.
Who's there?
Whoopi.
Whoopi who?
Whoopi cushion.

☆　☆　☆

Knock knock.
Who's there?
Wicked.
Wicked who?
Wicked make beautiful music
　　together.

Knock knock.
Who's there?
Wilde.
Wilde who?
Wilde at heart.

☆　☆　☆

Knock knock.
Who's there?
Wilfred.
Wilfred who?
Wilfred come if we ask nicely?

☆　☆　☆

Knock knock.
Who's there?
Will.
Will who?
Will you go away?

☆　☆　☆

Knock knock.
Who's there?
Willa.
Willa who?
Willa present make you happy?

Knock knock.
Who's there?
Wine.
Wine who?
Wine now you are all grown up!

Knock knock.
Who's there?
Winnie.
Winne who?
Winnie is better than losing.

Knock knock.
Who's there?
Witch.
Witch who?
Witch witch would you like it to be?

Knock knock.
Who's there?
Wizard.
Wizard who?
Wizard you I'm lost.

Knock knock.
Who's there?
Wooden shoe.
Wooden shoe who?
Wooden shoe like to know?

What happened when Dumbo went to a mind-reader?
They gave him his money back.

"Let me inform you, young man," said the slow elderly golfer, "that I was playing this game before you were born."
"That's all very well, but I'd be obliged if you'd try to finish it before I die."

☆　　☆　　☆

"I'd like you to accept my opinion for what it's worth."
"That means you owe me a cent."

☆　　☆　　☆

"You're only as old as you act."
"That means you're about six months old."

☆　　☆　　☆

Gordon: My wallet's full of big bills.
Graham: All unpaid, I expect.

☆　　☆　　☆

"Does your brother keep himself clean?"
"Oh, yes. He takes a bath every month whether he needs one or not."

Knock knock.
Who's there?
Woodworm.
Woodworm who?
Woodworm cake be enough or would
    you like two?

Knock knock.
Who's there?
Woody.
Woody who?
Woody come if we asked him?

Knock knock.
Who's there?
Woolf.
Woolf who?
Woolf in sheep's clothing.

Knock knock.
Who's there?
Worm.
Worm who?
Worm in here isn't it?

Knock knock.
Who's there?
Wyn.
Wyn who?
Wyn or lose, it's the taking part that
    counts.

Knock knock.
Who's there?
Wynona.
Wynona who?
Wynona short race.

Brian: Let's play a game of wits.
Diane: No, let's play something you can play too.

Comedian: Do you find me entertaining?
Friend: I'd say you were too dumb to entertain a thought.

Owen: Thank you so much for lending me that money. I shall be everlastingly in your debt.
Lenny: That's what I'm afraid of!

"I hear he's a very careful person."
"Well, he likes to economize on soap and water."

Bob had just missed a shot at goal, which meant the other team won. "I could kick myself," he groaned, as the players came off the pitch. "Don't bother," said the captain, "you'd miss."

"I hear she's a businesswoman."
"Yes, her nose is always in other people's business."

My friend is so stupid she thinks that an autograph is a chart showing sales figures for cars.

Why didn't the idiot play water polo when he was on holiday?
He couldn't get the horse into the water.

Pattie: I'd like a dress to match my eyes.
Mattie: Is it possible to buy a bloodshot dress?

Ryan: They say she's highly strung.
Brian: I always knew she reminded me of a badly tuned violin.

She's so ugly that even spiders run away when they see her.

Knock knock.
Who's there?
Yellow.
Yellow who?
Yellowver the din – I can't hear you.

☆　☆　☆

Knock knock.
Who's there?
Yoga.
Yoga who?
Yoga what it takes!

☆　☆　☆

Knock knock.
Who's there?
Xavier.
Xavier who?
Xavier breath! I'm not leaving.

☆　☆　☆

Knock knock.
Who's there?
York.
York who?
York, york, york. This is funny.

☆　☆　☆

Knock knock.
Who's there?
Xena.
Xena who?
Xena minute!

☆　☆　☆

Knock, knock.
Who's there?
Datsun.
Datsun who?
Datsun awful dress you're wearing!

Peggy: I'm going to thump Fred. He said I was stupid.
Peter: Don't take any notice of him. He's only repeating what everyone else says.

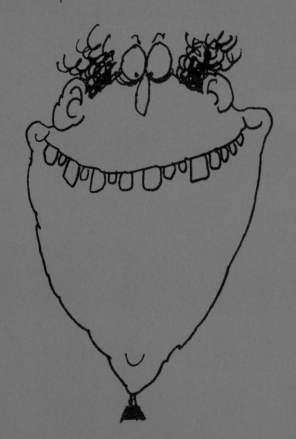

She only cooks health food – you have to be in perfect health in order to eat it and survive.

Fat Lady: I'd love to be able to lose weight, but I've no willpower.
Thin Lady: You're just a wishful shrinker.

Jemima: Remember I'm a big name in these parts.
Jonathan: Yes, "Thick and Stupid" is quite a mouthful.

Tammy: Did you like my curry?
Sammy: Did you buy it yourself?

"I've been told I have the face of a saint."
"Yes, a Saint Bernard."

"You smell like Dizzy."
"Dizzy who?"
"Dizzy Nfectant."

"Why do you say your uncle is spiteful?"
"Because when the doctor said he had rabies, he immediately wrote a list of people he wanted to bite."

Knock knock.
Who's there?
You.
You who?
Who's that calling out?

Knock knock.
Who's there?
Yul.
Yul who?
Yuletide.

Knock knock.
Who's there?
Yvette.
Yvette who?
Yvette helps lots of animals.

Knock knock.
Who's there?
Yvonne.
Yvonne who?
Yvonne to know vat you are doing.

Knock knock.
Who's there?
Zippy.
Zippy who?
Zippydidooda, zippydeeay!